STATE OF ALABAMA
DEPARTMENT OF ARCHIVES AND HISTORY
THOMAS M. OWEN, Director
Bulletin No. 5

Revolutionary Soldiers in Alabama

BEING A LIST OF NAMES, COMPILED FROM AUTHENTIC SOURCES, OF SOLDIERS OF THE AMERICAN REVOLUTION, WHO RESIDED IN THE STATE OF ALABAMA

Compiled by THOMAS M. OWEN

Southern Historical Press, Inc.
Greenville, South Carolina

This volume was reproduced from
An 1975 edition located in the
Publisher's private library,
Greenville, South Carolina

All rights reserved. No part of this publication may be reproduced,
stored in a retrieval system, transmitted in any form, posted
on to the web in any form or by any means without the
prior written permission of the publisher.

Please direct all correspondence and orders to:

www.southernhistoricalpress.com
or
SOUTHERN HISTORICAL PRESS, Inc.
PO BOX 1267
375 West Broad Street
Greenville, SC   29601
southernhistoricalpress@gmail.com

Originally published: Montgomery, AL. 1911
Reprinted by:
Southern Historical Press, Inc.
Greenville, SC
ISBN #0-89308-980-X
All rights Reserved.
Printed in the United States of America

PREFATORY NOTE.

It is believed that the publication of this compilation will be of much practical service to large numbers of people interested in a study of the personal records of the Heroes of the American Revolution. And this is true, although the lists are manifestly incomplete, and the sketches are wanting in many desirable details.

The lists have been made up from altogether reliable and authentic sources. These consist of contemporary obituaries, drawn from old newspaper files; the *Revolutionary Pension Roll,* published by the U. S. Government as Senate Document 514, 3 volumes, 23rd Congress, 1st Session, 1833-34; the *Census of Pensioners,* taken officially in 1840, and published by the U. S. Government in 1841, in one volume; inscriptions from tombstones; well authenticated data taken from published family histories; and the manuscript *Pension Book,* kept officially by the State Branch Bank at Mobile. A few other sources have been drawn upon. Citation of the authority or authorities has been given in each case.

In 1904 Mrs. P. H. Mell published a paper containing thirty sketches, entitled "Revolutionary Soldiers Buried in Alabama." It appears as pp. 527-572, Vol. iv, *Transactions* of the Alabama Historical Society, 1899-1903. Mrs. Mell had been State Historian of the Alabama Division of the Daughters of the American Revolution. While limited in numbers, her paper was prepared with great care. The sketches appear in their proper places in the list here presented, with due credit. Although a few lists of names, either by counties or localities, had been compiled, no pretentious effort, prior to the work of Mrs. Mell, had been undertaken.

Inasmuch as this is but a preliminary effort looking to a complete and exhaustive record, the attention of the Department should be brought to any and all errors, to dates and places of death, to places of burial, to the names of those who removed from the State, and to all others whose names ought to be included.

Montgomery, Ala., Sept. 30, 1910.

Alphabetical List of Revolutionary Soldiers in Alabama

ADAMS, BRYANT, a resident of Montgomery county; private, particular service not shown; enrolled on September 26, 1834, under act of Congress of June 7, 1832, payment to date from March 4, 1831; annual allowance, $30; transferred to North Carolina, letter August 29, 1836.—*Pension Book, State Branch Bank, Mobile.*

AGNEW, GEORGE, a resident of Lauderdale county; private in cavalry, particular service not shown; enrolled on September 29, 1836, under act of Congress of June 7, 1832, payment to date from March 4, 1831; annual allowance, $25.—*Pension Book, State Branch Bank, Mobile.*

ALEXANDER, ——, aged 98, resided in Mobile county, June 1, 1840; no facts given.—*Census of Pensioners,* 1841. p. 149.

ALEXANDER, ASA, aged 74, and a resident of Dale county; private Georgia Militia; enrolled on June 17, 1833, under act of Congress of June 7, 1832, payment to date from March 4, 1831; annual allowance, $80; sums received up to date of publication of list, $200.—*Revolutionary Pension Roll,* in vol. xiv, Sen. Doc. 514, 23rd Con., 1st sess., 1833-34.

ALEXANDER, JEREMIAH, aged 113 (evidently an error for 71), and a resident of Morgan county; private Massachusetts Militia State Troops; enrolled on September 17, 1833, under act of Congress of June 7, 1832, payment to date from March 4, 1831; annual allowance, $33.33; sums received to date of publication of list, $83.32.—*Revolutionary Pension Roll,* in Vol. xiv, Sen. Doc. 514, 23rd Cong., 1st sess., 1833-34. He resided in Walker county, June 1, 1840, aged 76.—*Census of Pensioners,* 1841, p. 150.

ALLEN, DAVID, a resident of Franklin county; private, particular service not shown; enrolled on March 8, 1833, under act of Congress of June 7, 1832, payment to date from September 4, 1833; annual allowance, $60.—*Pension Book, State Branch Bank, Mobile.*

ALLEN, EDWARD, aged 75, and a resident of Franklin county; private N. C. Continental Line; enrolled on March 8, 1833, under act of Congress of June 7, 1832, payment to date from March 4, 1831; annual allowance, $60; sums received up to date of publication of list, $180.—*Revolutionary Pension Roll*, in Vol. xiv, Sen. Doc. 514, 23rd Cong., 1st sess., 1833-34.

ALLEN, ROBERT, "DEATH—Another Old Soldier of the Revolution gone home. Died on the 29th ult. Robert Allen, of this county. They leave us one by one—yet they live in our memory."—*The Democrat*, Huntsville, Ala., November 3, 1826.

ALLEN, ROBERT, aged 66, and a resident of Madison county; Sergeant Virginia Continental Line; enrolled on January 29, 1824, under act of Congress of March 18, 1818, payment to date from October 26, 1823; annual allowance, $96; sums received to date of publication of list, $213.54.—*Revolutionary Pension Roll*, in Vol. xiv, Sen. Doc. 514, 23rd Cong., 1st sess., 1833-34.

ALSOBROOK, JESSE, aged 72, and a resident of Greene county; private N. C. Militia; enrolled on March 26, 1833, under act of Congress of June 7, 1832, payment to date from March 4, 1831; annual allowance, $50; sums received to date of publiaction of list, $100.—*Revolutionary Pension Roll*, in Vol. xiv, Sen. Doc. 514, 23rd Cong., 1st sess., 1833-34. He resided in Sumter county, June 1, 1840, aged 77.—*Census of Pensioners*, 1841, p. 149.

AMINET, JOHN, aged 81, and a resident of Madison county, private Virginia Continental Line; enrolled on January 5, 1833, under act of Congress of June 7, 1832, payment received to date from March 4, 1831; annual allowance, $80. —*Revolutionary Pension Roll*, in Vol. xiv, Sen. Doc. 514, 23rd Cong., 1st sess., 1833-34.

The Democrat, Huntsville, April 11, 1833, contains the following obituary:

"Suddenly at his residence in this County, on the 30th of March, Mr. John Amonit, in the Eighty-second year of his age—thus another revolutionary spirit has sunk into its rest— Rarely are we called to record the death of a more virtuous man.—He has been a citizen of this county upwards of twenty years. In the domestic circle, he was a kind and tender father, and affectionate companion, a social and obliging neighbor, much beloved by numerous friends, and enemies he had none. In youth, he boldly met the foe and nobly defended the cause of liberty—few have ever so well prepared for their last great change—he settled his earthly concerns—ate a hearty supper—called his family around him—addressed the throne of grace—lay down in perfect composure—fell asleep in the arms of his Saviour, and awoke in the Paradise of his God. Thus died Mr. Amonit, without a groan, and left a wife, four children and numerous friends to mourn their loss, which is his infinite gain, and he now reaps the just reward of his labors."

ARMISTEAD, WILLIAM. The grave of this soldier is described in Ball's *Clark County, Alabama*, pp. 475-6. We learn that a Capt. William Armistead of Virginia and three sons, Robert, Westwood and John, became citizens of Clarke. The father was a man of strong peculiarities, a gentleman of the old school, wearing knee buckles and retaining English tastes. He was twice married and had three sons and three daughters. One daughter married John Morriss, in North Carolina, and moved to Alabama; another daughter married Edmund Waddell, in North Carolina; the third married Dr. Neal Smith, a gentleman of prominence in his day.

The grave stands alone, neatly enclosed with rocks and pickets on a hill near Amity church in the family burial ground, on the plantation bequeathed by him to his son-in-law, Dr. Neal Smith, about eight miles from Grove Hill.

The following is a copy from the marble slab:

In
memory of
CAPTAIN WILLIAM ARMISTEAD,
a soldier of the
Revolution, a native
of Virginia,
who departed this life
March 1st, 1842,
aged 80 years.

He resided in Clarke County, June 1, 1840.—*Census of Pensioners*, 1841, p. 149.—Mrs. P. H. Mell, in *Transactions* of the Alabama Historical Society, vol. iv, pp. 529-533, has an extended sketch, with genealogical notes, etc.

ARNOLD, THOMAS, aged 71, and a resident of Autauga county; private N. C. Continental Line; enrolled on Jan. 4,

1834, under act of Congress of June 7, 1832, payment to date from March 4, 1831; annual allowance, $30; sums received to date of publication of list, $90.—*Revolutionary Pension Roll,* in Vol. xiv, Sen. Doc. 514, 23rd Cong., 1st sess., 1833-34.

BACON, RICHARD, aged 73, and a resident of Madison county; private and commissary Virginia Continental Line; enrolled on December 31, 1832, under act of Congress of June 7, 1832, payment to date from March 4, 1831; annual allowance, $73.33.—*Revolutionary Pension Roll,* in Vol. xiv, Sen. Doc. 514, 23rd Cong., 1st sess., 1833-34.

BAGWELL, FREDERICK, a resident of Fayette county; private, particular service not shown; enrolled on August 20, 1835, under act of Congress of June 7, 1832, payment to date from March 4, 1831; annual allowance, $50.—*Pension Book,* State Branch Bank, Mobile. He resided in Fayette county, June 1, 1840, aged 80.—*Census of Pensioners,* 1841, p. 148.

BAILES, ELDRIDGE, aged 74, and a resident of Madison county; private S. C. Continental Line; enrolled on January 24, 1833, under act of Congress of June 7, 1832, payment to date from March 4, 1831; annual allowance, $75; sums received to date of publication of list, $225.—*Revolutionary Pension Roll,* in Vol. xiv, Sen. Doc. 514, 23rd Cong., 1st sess., 1833-34.

BAILY, MOSES, aged 79, and a resident of Madison county; private Virginia Continental Line; enrolled on January 24, 1833, under act of Congress of June 7, 1832; payment to date from March 4, 1831; annual allowance, $80; sums received to date of publication of list, $240.—*Revolutionary Pension Roll,* in Vol. xiv, Sen. Doc. 514, 23rd Cong., 1st sess., 1833-34.

BAILY, REUBEN, aged .70, and a resident of Limestone county; private S. C. Continental Line; enrolled on April 25, 1825, under act of Congress of March 18, 1818, payment to date from March 4, 1825; annual allowance, $96; sums received to date of publication of list, $240; died.—*Revolutionary Pension Roll,* in Vol. xiv, Sen. Doc. 514, 23rd Cong., 1st sess., 1833-34.

BAKER, SAMUEL, private, particular service not shown; enrolled on February 19, 1835, under act of Congress of June 7, 1832, payment to date from March 4, 1831; annual allowance, $20; removed to Kentucky.—*Pension Book,* State Branch Bank, Mobile.

Revolutionary Soldiers in Alabama. 9

BALLENGER, JOHN, aged 75, and a resident of St. Clair county; private Maryland Militia; enrolled on September 20, 1833, under act of Congress of June 7, 1832, payment to date from March 4, 1831; annual allowance, $80; sums received to date of publication of list, $240.—*Revolutionary Pension Roll,* in Vol. xiv, Sen. Doc. 514, 23rd Cong., 1st sess., 1833-34.

BARCLAY, ROBERT. "Departed this life on the 26th July, 1848, *Robert Barclay,* aged 85 years; born Nov. 1763, in Ireland; came with his father to South Carolina in 1769; served as a private soldier under Sumpter towards the close of the War of the Revolution, and emigrated to Tennessee in 1802, and afterwards to Morgan County, Alabama, in 1816, where he died; being one of the first pioneers who crossed the Tennessee River in Alabama. He was remarkably healthy, never having any sickness until worn out with age; even retaining his eyesight to the last, never using a pair of spectacles; he professed religion and joined the Baptist Church after coming to Morgan County, and has left three sons and three daughters to mourn his loss. Thus has fallen the last revolutionary patriot that we are acquainted with; tho' there are doubtlesss many more; but the time is close at hand when the last patriot that bared his bosom to the enemies of American freedom, will cease to live on earth; but the time should be long before a memory of their deeds should be lost to their survivors.—*The Democrat,* Huntsville, August 9, 1848. He resided in Morgan County, June 1, 1840.—*Census of Pensioners,* 1841, p. 148.

BARNETT, THOMAS, aged 70, and a resident of Perry county; private S. C. Militia; enrolled on November 4, 1833, under act of Congress of June 7, 1832, payment to date from March 4, 1831; annual allowance, $20; sums received to date of publication of list, $60.—*Revolutionary Pension Roll,* in Vol. xiv, Sen. Doc. 514, 23rd Cong., 1st sess., 1833-34.

BARTLEY, ROBERT, aged 72, and a resident of Morgan county; private S. C. Continental Line; enrolled on July 2, 1833, under act of Congress of June 7, 1832, payment to date from March 4, 1831; annual allowance, $36.66; sums received to date of publication of list, $109.98.—*Revolutionary Pension Roll,* in Vol. xiv, Sen. Doc. 514, 23rd Cong., 1st sess., 1833-34.

BATTLES, NOEL, aged 80, and a resident of St. Clair county; private Virginia Continental Line and Militia; enrolled on September 29, 1833, under act of Congress of June

10   Department of Archives and History.

7, 1832; payment to date from March 4, 1831; annual allowance, $80; sums received to date of publication of list, $240.—*Revolutionary Pension Roll,* in Vol. xiv, Sen. Doc. 514, 23rd Cong., 1st sess., 1833-34. He resided in St. Clair county, June 1, 1840, with William Battles; aged 100.—*Census of Pensioners,* 1841, p. 148.

BAXTER, JOHN, age not given, a resident of Dallas county; private Irwin's Regiment; date of enrollment not given; payment to date from September 4, 1818; annual allowance, $36.80; sums received to date of publication of list, $460; transferred from N. C. from March 4, 1821. Died.—*Revolutionary Pension Roll,* in Vol. xiv, Sen. Doc. 514, 23rd Cong., 1st sess., 1833-34.

BAYLIS, HEZEKIAH, aged 77, and a resident of Madison county; private Virginia Militia; enrolled on January 24, 1833, under act of Congress of June 7, 1832, payment to date from March 4, 1831; annual alowance, $20.—*Revolutionary Pension Roll,* in Vol. xiv, Sen. Doc. 514, 23rd Cong., 1st sess., 1833-34.

BECK, ANDREW, aged 79, and a resident of Perry county; private N. C. Militia; enrolled on September 29, 1833, under act of Congress of June 7, 1832, payment to date from March 4, 1831; annual allowance, $20.—*Revolutionary Pension Roll,* in Vol. xiv, Sen. Doc. 514, 23rd Cong., 1st sess., 1833-34.

BEESON, EDWARD, aged 75, and a resident of St. Clair county; capt. and lieut. N. C. State Troops, enrolled on September 29, 1833, under act of Congress of June 7, 1832, payment to date from March 4, 1831; annual allowance, $180; sums received to date of publication of list, $540.—*Revolutionary Pension Roll,* in Vol. xiv, Sen. Doc. 514, 23rd Cong., 1st sess., 1833-34.

BENTLEY, EFFORD, aged 74, and a resident of Madison county; private and sergeant Virginia Militia; enrolled on May 2, 1833, under act of Congress of June 7, 1832; payment to date from March 4, 1831; annual allowance, $44.10; sums received to date of publication of list, $110.25.—*Revolutionary Pension Roll,* in Vol. xiv, Sen. Doc. 514, 23rd Cong., 1st sess., 1833-34.

BEVERS, JAMES, aged 73, and a resident of Limestone county; private Virginia Continental Line; enrolled on De-

Revolutionary Soldiers in Alabama. 11

cember 11, 1823, under act of Congress of March 18, 1818, payment to date from October 20, 1823; annual allowance, $96; sums received to date of publication of list, $275.08. Died December, 1826.—*Revolutionary Pension Roll,* in Vol. xiv, Sen. Doc. 514, 23rd Cong., 1st sess., 1833-34.

BEVILLE, EDWARD, aged 74, and a resident of Madison county; private Virginia Continental Line; enrolled on January 5, 1833, under act of Congress of June 7, 1832, payment to date from March 4, 1831; annual allowance, $36.66; sums received to date of publication of list, $91.65.—*Revolutionary Pension Roll,* in Vol. xiv, Sen. Doc. 513, 23rd Cong., 1st sess., 1833-34. He resided in Madison county, June 1, 1840, aged 78.—*Census of Pensioners,* 1841, p. 148.

"DIED—On the 15th of March, 1847, at her residence in Madison county, Ala., *Mary Beville,* in the 84th year of her age. And on the 20th of September, 1847, *Edward Beville,* Sen., her husband, died at the same place, in the 88th year of his age. They emigrated from Virginia, Mecklinburg county, to North Carolina, about the year 1805, and from there to this county about 1823. Edward Beville, Sen., was a soldier in the Revolutionary war, and drew a pension at the time of his death; he was a great lover of liberty, and often spoke of the prosperity of his country. The writer has been acquainted with him for the last 15 or 20 years—he was strictly honest and a great lover of truth, respected and esteemed by all who knew him. O. R.—*The Democrat,* Huntsville, October 27, 1847.

BILLINGSLEY, CLEMENT, aged 84, resided in Autauga county, June 1, 1840.—*Census of Pensioners,* 1841, p. 149.

BIRD, JOHN, private, particular service not shown; enrolled on January 10, 1837, under act of Congress of June 7, 1832; annual allowance, $23.33; no record of any payment having been made.—*Pension Book,* State Branch Bank, Mobile.

BISHOP, WYATT, aged 76, and a resident of Franklin county; private Virginia Militia; enrolled on November 15, 1833, under act of Congress of June 7, 1832, payment to date from March 4, 1831; annual allowance, $36.66; sums received to date of publication of list, $109.98.—*Revolutionary Pension Roll,* in Vol. xiv, Sen. Doc. 514, 23rd Cong., 1st sess., 1833-34.

BLACK, DAVID, aged 80, resided in Fayette county, June 1, 1840—*Census of Pensioners,* 1841, p. 148.

BLACK, JAMES, aged 74, and a resident of Greene county; private N. C. Continental Line; enrolled on July 2, 1833, under act of Congress of June 7, 1832, payment to date from March 4, 1831; annual allowance, $60.80; sums received to date of publication of list, $180.—*Revolutionary Pension Roll*, in Vol. xiv, Sen. Doc. 514, 23rd Cong., 1st sess., 1833-34.

BLACKBURN, BENJAMIN, age not given, a resident of Tuscaloosa county; private Lewis's Regiment; date of enrollment not given, payment to date from April 1, 1810; annual allowance, $60; sums received, $363.90; transferred from Tennessee from September 4, 1819; or April 24, 1816, rate increased to annual allowance of $96, under which the sum of $1,715.18 received to date of publication of list.—*Revolutionary Pension Roll*, in Vol. xiv, Sen. Doc. 514, 23rd Cong., 1st sess., 1833-34.

BLACKBOURN, CLEMENT, aged 80, resided in Madison county, June 1, 1840.—*Census of Pensioners*, 1841, p. 148.

BLAKELY, AQUILLA, aged 94, and a resident of Blount county; private and sergeant Virginia Militia; enrolled on July 2, 1833, under act of Congress of June 7, 1832, payment to date from March 4, 1831; annual allowance, $35; sums received to date of publication of list, $105.—*Revolutionary Pension Roll*, in Part 3, Vol. xiii, Sen. Doc. 514, 23rd Cong., 1st sess., 1833-34.

BLANKENSHIP, REUBEN, aged 69, and a resident of Shelby county; private Virginia Militia; enrolled on May 24, 1833, under act of Congress of June 7, 1832, payment to date from March 4, 1831; annual allowance, $23.31.—*Revolutionary Pension Roll*, in Vol. xiv, Sen. Doc. 514, 23rd Cong., 1st sess., 1833-34. He resided in Coosa county, June 1, 1840, aged 73.—*Census of Pensioners*, 1841, p. 149. He was buried at Poplar Springs church in that county.—D. B. Oden, of Childersburg, Ala., in *Transactions* of the Alabama Historical Society, Vol. iv, p. 533.

BODLY, JOHN, aged 72, and a resident of Jackson county; private S. C. State Troops and Militia; enrolled on January 22, 1834, under act of Congress of June 7, 1832, payment to date from March 4, 1831; annual allowance, $80; sums received to date of publication of list, $240.—*Revolutionary Pension Roll*, in Vol. xiv, Sen. Doc. 514, 23rd Cong., 1st sess., 1833-34.

Revolutionary Soldiers in Alabama. 13

BOLTON, BENJAMIN, aged 69, and a resident of Dallas county; private N. C. Continental Line; enrolled on January 21, 1822, under act of Congress of March 18, 1818, payment to date from September 15, 1820; annual allowance, $96; sums received to date of publication of list, $1,245.32.—*Revolutionary Pension Roll,* in Vol. xiv, Sen. Doc. 514, 23rd Cong., 1st sess., 1833-34.

BOYD, JAMES, a resident of Jefferson county; private, particular service not shown; enrolled on September 17, 1834, under act of Congress of June 7, 1832, payment to date from March 4, 1831; annual allowance, $23.33.—*Pension Book,* State Branch Bank, Mobile.

BOYDSTON, SAMUEL, aged 72, and a resident of Perry county; private Tennessee Militia; enrolled on September 17, 1833, under act of Congress of June 7, 1832; payment to date from March 4, 1831; annual allowance, $46.66; sums received to date of publication of list, $116.65.—*Revolutionary Pension Roll,* in Vol. xiv, Sen. Doc. 514, 23rd Cong., 1st 1833-34.

BRADFORD, THOMAS.—"Not so many miles north of Amity church, on this same Choctaw line, stands the grave and memorial stone of another Revolutionary soldier.

"THOMAS BRADFORD.—A slight enclosure surrounds this lone burial spot, and the headstone, with its few and simple words, reminds every passer-by of man's mortality, and also that the dust is sleeping there of one of the soldiers of '76, the Immortal Band of whom a South Carolina patriot, and eloquent Christian lawyer, asks the touching, the thrilling question, 'Shall they meet again in the amaranthine bowers of spotless purity, of perfect bliss, of eternal glory?'

"Thomas Bradford had two sons, Brasil and Nathan."—Rev. T. H. Ball's *Clarke County, Alabama,* p. 476.

BRAGG, PETER M., SR.—"OBITUARY—Departed this life, at his residence in Lowndes county, Ala., on the 21st of May, *Mr. Peter N. Bragg, Sr.,* A SOLDIER OF THE REVOLUTION, at the advanced age of 78 years.

"Mr. Bragg was a native of Virginia, born in Fauquier county March 4th, 1763; he entered the American Army under command of Gen. Greene, at the early age of 16; and was in two distinguished battles—that of Guilford Court House, N. C., and the one near Camden, S. C.

"At the close of the war, Mr. Bragg removed to Spartanburg District, S. C., where he resided about forty-six years, and moved thence, in December 1829, to Lowndes county, Ala., where he continued till his death. He was a member of the Baptist church more than 40 years; and his irreproachable life and unstained character exemplify the honesty of his profession and the purity of his heart. He was no partizan in religious matters, but taking the Bible alone, as his standard of Christian profession and practice; he bowed to no other tribunal. If he ever erred it was an error of the judgment, not of heart. And it may fairly demand a doubt, whether in his degenerate age, any man ever lived more studiously the life of a Christian. To speak in terms most appropriate, of the domestic, social and moral worth of Peter N. Bragg in the narrow space assigned in Obituary, would be, to those who knew him, but slight praise, and only show the imbecility of a few presuming lines, which attempt to declare the virtuous acts and beneficent deeds characteristic of a long, industrious, enterprising and virtuous life; but let it suffice here to observe, that Mr. Bragg lived for his country, his fellow-man and his God.

"As a neighbor, he promptly discharged all the duties which the mutual obligation and reciprocal dependencies of society demand.

"As a citizen, he freely took part in all matters affecting our civil rights and municipal happiness. As a Christian, he was attentive and liberal to the indigent, merciful and humane to the afflicted, kind and hospitable to strangers, and just and merciful to all."—*The Greenville Mountaineer*, Greenville, S. C., June 12, 1841.

BRADLEY, JOHN, Sen., aged 83, resided in Clarke county, June 1, 1840.—*Census of Pensioners*, 1841, p. 149.

BRADLEY, JOHN, Sen., aged 83, resided in Marshall county, June 1, 1840.—*Census of Pensioners*, 1841, p. 148.

BREWER, BARNET, aged 71, and a resident of Montgomery county; private Virginia Militia; enrolled on June 15, 1834, under act of Congress of June 7, 1832, payment to date from March 4, 1831; annual allowance, $20.—*Revolutionary Pension Roll*, in Vol. xiv, Sen. Doc. 514, 23rd Cong., 1st sess., 1833-34. He resided in Macon county, June 1, 1840, aged 77.—*Census of Pensioners*, 1841, p. 149.

BROUGHTON, THOMAS, sergeant and lieutenant; particular service not shown, deceased; records show that his widow, Mary Broughton, lived within the vicinity of Decatur

Revolutionary Soldiers in Alabama. 15

and received payment from that branch of the State Bank.—*Pension Book,* State Branch Bank, Mobile.

BROWN, HAMILTON, aged 79, and a resident of Greene county, private S. C. Militia; enrolled on September 17, 1833, under act of Congress of June 7, 1832, payment to date from March 4, 1831; annual allowance, $80; sums received to date of publication of list, $240.—*Revolutionary Pension Roll,* in Vol. xiv, Sen. Doc. 14, 23rd Cong., 1st sess., 1833-34. He resided in Greene county, June 1, 1840, aged 86.—*Census of Pensioners,* 1841, p. 149.

BROWN, JOHN, a resident of Jefferson county; private, particular service not shown; enrolled on March 15, 1833, under act of Congress of June 7, 1832, payment to date from September 4, 1833; annual allowance, $80.66.—*Pension Book,* State Branch Bank, Mobile.

BROWN, WILLIAM, aged 88, resided in Dallas County, June 1, 1840.—*Census of Pensioners,* 1841, p. 149.

BRUTON, BENJAMIN, aged 73, and a resident of Tuscaloosa county; private and sergeant N. C. Militia; enrolled on April 23, 1833, under act of Congress of June 7, 1832, payment to date from March 4, 1831; annual allowance, $53.33; sums received to date of publication of list, $133.32.—*Revolutionary Pension Roll,* in Vol. xiv, Sen. Doc. 514, 23rd Cong., 1st sess., 1833-34.

BRYANT, ELIZABETH, aged 71, resided in Jackson county, June 1, 1840, with H. M. Bryant.—*Census of Pensioners,* 1841, p. 148.

BRYANT, JOHN, aged 85, resided in Jackson county, June 1, 1840.—*Census of Pensioners,* 1841, p. 148.

BURFORD, JOHN, Sen., aged 75, and a resident of Jefferson county; private and sergeant N. C. Continental Line; enrolled on November 15, 1833, under act of Congress of June 7, 1832, payment to date from March 4, 1831; annual allowance, 43.88.—*Revolutionary Pension Roll,* in Vol. xiv, Sen. Doc. 514, 23rd Cong., 1st sess., 1833-34.

BUTLER, JAMES, a resident of Shelby county; private, particular service not shown; enrolled on February 22, 1833, under act of Congress of June 7, 1832, payment to date from September 4, 1836; annual allowance, $73.33.—*Pension Book,* State Branch Bank, Mobile. He resided in Shelby county, June 1, 1840, aged 83.—*Census of Pensioners,* 1841, p. 149.

BUTLER, WILLIAM, aged 78, and a resident of Lawrence county; private Virginia Militia; enrolled on November 4, 1833, under act of Congress of June 7, 1832, payment to date from March 4, 1831; annual allowance, $43.33.—*Revolutionary Pension Roll,* in Vol. xiv, Sen. Doc. 514, 23rd Cong., 1st sess., 1833-34.

BUZBEE, JACOB, aged 74, and a resident of St. Clair county; Private S. C. Militia; enrolled on March 6, 1834, under act of Congress of June 7, 1832, payment to date from March 4, 1831; annual allowance, $63.33; sums received to date of publication of list, $189.99.—*Revolutionary Pension Roll,* in Vol. xiv, Sen. Doc. 514, 23rd Cong., 1st sess., 1833-34.

CADENHEAD, JAMES, Sen., aged 98, resided in Pike county, June 1, 1840.—*Census of Pensioners,* 1841, p. 149.

CAFFEY, JOHN. The *Alabama Journal,* Montgomery, August 28, 1826, contains the obituary of John Caffey:

"Died, at his plantation, in the vicinity of Montgomery, on Saturday, the 19th, inst. (Aug. 19, 1826), of bilious fever, Mr. John Caffey, in seventy-fifth year of his age.

"Mr. Caffey was born on the eastern shore of Maryland. At an early period of the revolution he enlisted under the command of Washington and La Fayette. After the struggle for independence was over he settled in Guilford county, N. C., where he had the confidence of his fellow citizens. He moved to this town in 1817 and was esteemed for his peaceful and neighborly conduct. Mr. Caffey had long been an exemplary member of the church, and when sensible his last moments were approaching, he surrendered his spirit with praises of God on his lips and an entire possession of his understanding."

He was the son of Michael Caffey of North Ireland, who migrated to New Jersey early in the 18th century. His wife was Mary Buchanan of Virginia. Mr. William Hardwick Ruth, a great-great-grandson now (1910) resides in Montgomery.

His remains lie in an old family burying ground on the Woodley road, near the city of Montgomery. He was the friend of Lafayette, and when that distinguished patriot visited Montgomery in 1825, one of the old veterans to greet him was John Caffey.—See Blue's *Montgomery Directory,* 1878; and *Archives of Maryland,* Vol. 18, p. 27 and 643.

CALDWELL, DAVID, aged 87, resided in Talladega county, June 1, 1840, with Charles Caldwell.—*Census of Pensioners,* 1841, p. 148.

Revolutionary Soldiers in Alabama. 17

CALDWELL, JAMES. Mrs. P. H. Mell in *Transactions* of the Alabama Historical Society, vol. iv, pp. 534-5, says:

"James Caldwell is buried in the cemetery at old Davisville, in Calhoun county, Ala., one and one-half miles south of Iron City station, twelve miles east of Anniston, on the Southern railroad. The 'oldest inhabitant' could give no information concerning the soldier.

"The tomb is built of brick; about 8 feet long, 6½ feet wide, and 5 feet high. The shingles of the roofs are badly rotted. A plain marble tablet is let into the wall of the tomb, bearing this inscription:

Sacred
to the memory of
JAMES CALDWELL,
who died October 2nd,
1847;
in the 98th year
of his age.
He was a soldier of the Revolution.

"The above account was furnished by W. B. Bowling, of Lafayette, Ala.

"Efforts have been made in vain to find the history of this old soldier. It is said that he came from South Carolina. He is another one of those forgotten heroes whose graves are scattered over the State."

CAMPBELL, CHARLES, aged 76, and a resident of Lauderdale county; private Virginia State Troops; enrolled on October 7, 1833, under act of Congress of June 7, 1832, payment to date from March 4, 1831; annual allowance, $80.—*Revolutionary Pension Roll*, in Vol. xiv, Sen. Doc. 514, 23rd Cong., 1st sess., 1833-34.

CAMPBELL, DAVID, aged 72, and a resident of Greene county; private S. C. Militia; enrolled on September 17, 1833, under act of Congress of June 7, 1832, payment to date from March 4, 1831; annual allowance, $30; sums received to date of publication of list, $90.—*Revolutionary Pension Roll*, in Vol. xiv, Sen. Doc. 514, 23rd Cong., 1st sess., 1833-34. He resided in Greene County, June 1, 1840, aged 80.—*Census of Pensioners*, 1841, p. 149.

CAMPBELL, GEORGE, a resident of Autauga county; private and sergeant, particular service not shown; enrolled on April 8, 1835, under act of Congress of June 7, 1832, payment to date from March 4, 1831; annual allowance, $55.83.—*Pension Book*, State Branch Bank, Mobile.

CARD, HUGH, aged 84, resided in Randolph, June 1, 1840.—*Census of Pensioners,* 1841, p. 148.

CARGILL, THOMAS, age not given, a resident of Jackson county; private of Cavalry N. C. Militia; enrolled on January 6, 1834; under act of Congress of June 7, 1832, payment to date from March 4, 1831; annual allowance, $100; sums received to date of publication of list, $300.—*Revolutionary Pension Roll,* in Vol. xiv, Sen. Doc. 514, 23rd Cong., 1st sess., 1833-34. He resided in Marshall county, June 1, 1840, aged 77.—*Census of Pensioners,* 1841, p. 148.

CARROL, DUMPSEY, aged 82, and a resident of Wilcox county; private N. C. Militia; enrolled on July 25, 1834, under act of Congress of June 7, 1832, payment to date from March 4, 1831; annual allowance, $20.—*Revolutionary Pension Roll,* in Vol. xiv, Sen. Doc. 514, 23rd Cong., 1st sess., 1833-34.

CARROLL, DEMPSEY, aged 78, resided in Wilcox county, June 1, 1840.—*Census of Pensioners,* 1841, p. 149. (Probably same as preceding, but age of each makes it uncertain.)

CARUTHERS, HUGH, aged 77, and a resident of Madison county; private N. C. Continental Line; enrolled on December 31, 1832, under act of Congress of June 7, 1832, payment to date from March 4, 1831; annual allowance, $80; sums received to date of publication of list, $240.—*Revolutionary Pension Roll,* in Vol. xiv, Sen. Doc. 514, 23rd Cong., 1st sess., 1833-34.

CASEY, WILLIAM, aged 77, and a resident of Autauga county; private S. C. Militia; enrolled on March 7, 1834, under act of Congress of June 7, 1832; payment to date from March 4, 1831; annual allowance, $40.—*Revolutionary Pension Roll,* in Part 3, Vol. xiii, Sen. Doc. 514, 23rd Cong., 1st sess., 1833-34. He resided in Coosa county, June 1, 1840, with M. B. Casey, aged 89.—*Census of Pensioners,* 1841, p. 149.

CATCHUM, HUGH, aged 72, and a resident of Limestone county; private N. C. Militia and State Troops; enrolled on January 24, 1833, under act of Congress of June 7, 1832, payment to date from March 4, 1831; annual allowance, $46.66; sums received to date of publication of list, $139.98.—*Revolutionary Pension Roll,* in Vol. xiv, Sen. Doc. 514, 23rd Cong., 1st sess., 1833-34.

CAULK, JACOB, aged 85, resided in Madison county, June 1, 1840, with John H. Webster.—*Census of Pensioners,* 1841, p. 148.

CHANCELLOR, JERRY. "This soldier of the Revolution is buried in a country churchyard at Pine Level Methodist church, in Autauga county, eighteen miles west of Montgomery.

"A short sketch of the life of Jerry Chancellor may be found in the *Memorial Record of Alabama,* vol. ii., p. 895. He was born in England and came to America with his father and two brothers, when sixteen years of age. This was during the Revolutionary war. After remaining a short time in Virginia, the father and his two oldest sons, William and Jerry, came to South Carolina, leaving the youngest son, Jackson Chancellor, in Virginia. Tradition says that Chancellorsville, Virginia, was named for the family of this youngest son.

"When the Chancellors arrived in South Carolina they found the war raging violently all around them and it became necessary for them to decide what their own course should be. The father, whose loyalty to England could not be shaken, told his sons that he should join the British; the sons declared that they admired the Americans for standing up for their rights and they intended to cast their lots with the people of their adopted country. The father and sons never met again, but fought on opposite sides until the close of the Revolutionary war. We do not know in what regiment Jerry Chancellor served, but Saffell's *Records,* p. 293, states that Nov. 1, 1779, William Chancellor was a private in the South Carolina regiment commanded by Lieut. Col. Francis Marion, Seventh Company, Thomas Dunbar, captain.

"Jerry Chancellor married Galatea Gilbert and settled in South Carolina after the Revolution, where he remained until 1818, when he organized a colony in South Carolina and came with them to Alabama. They settled on the Autauga side of the Alabama river. He remained with this colony until his death. Descendants of Jerry Chancellor are now living in Childersburg and in Coosa county. His grandson, William S. Chancellor, was one of the oldest Masons in Alabama."—Mrs. P. H. Mell in *Transactions* of the Alabama Historical Society, Vol. iv., p. 535.

CHANDLER, JOHN, aged 89, resided in Benton county, June 1, 1840.—*Census of Pensioners,* 1841, p. 148.

CHERRY, JOSIAH, aged 79, resided in Marengo county, June 1, 1840, with J. W. Cherry.—*Census of Pensioners, 1841, p. 149.*

CLARKE, LEWIS, aged 71, and a resident of Jackson county; private Virginia Militia; enrolled on November 4, 1833, under the act of Congress of June 7, 1832, payment to date from March 4, 1831; annual allowance, $20.—*Revolutionary Pension Roll,* in Vol. xiv, Sen. Doc. 514, 23rd Cong., 1st sess., 1833-34. He resided in Jackson county, June 1, 1840, aged 77.—*Census of Pensioners, 1841, p. 148.*

CLARKE, THOMAS, aged 79, and a resident of Tuscaloosa county; private N. C. Militia; enrolled on September 26, 1833, under act of Congress of June 7, 1832, payment to date from March 4, 1831; annual allowance, $60; sums received to date of publication of list, $180.—*Revolutionary Pension Roll,* in Vol. xiv, Sen. Doc. 514, 23rd Cong., 1st sess., 1833-34.

CLICK, JOHN, resided in Jefferson county, on the East side of Valley Creek, between the present Powderly and old Hawkins Big Spring. Here he built a mill, which later became the property of his son, Moss Click.

CLOWER, JONATHAN, aged 71, and a resident of Bibb county; private N. Carolina Militia; enrolled on July 6, 1834, under act of Congress of June 7, 1832, payment to date from March 4, 1831; annual allowance, $40.—*Revolutionary Pension Roll,* in Part 3, Vol. xiii, Sen. Doc. 514, 23rd Cong., 1st sess., 1833-34.

COCHRAN, WILLIAM, age not given, a resident of Clarke county; sergeant Virginia Continental Line; enrolled on September 22, 1819, under act of Congress of March 18, 1818, payment to date from September 7, 1818; annual allowance, $96.; sums received to date of publication of list, $121.60; died December 12, 1819.—*Revolutionary Pension Roll,* in Vol. xiv, Sen. Doc. 514, 23rd Cong., 1st sess., 1833-34.

COLEMAN, CHARLES P., aged 71, and a resident of Greene county; private N. C. State Troops; enrolled on October 3, 1833, under act of Congress of June 7, 1832, payment to date from March 4, 1831; annual allowance, $80; sums received to date of publication of list, $240.—*Revolutionary Pension Roll,* in Vol. xiv, Sen. Doc. 514, 23rd Cong., 1st sess., 1833-34.

COLLIER, JAMES. DIED—At his residence near the village, on Monday the 20th instant, after a severe illness of two weeks, Mr. *James Collier,* in the 77th year of his age. Mr. Collier was a native of Virginia, and at an early period of his life entered the Revolutionary Army. Through the whole of that arduous and protracted struggle for liberty, he manifested the most untiring zeal and unceasing devotion in the cause of his country. He was no less distinguished for his patriotism, than for high-toned honor and those bland and social virtues which endeared him to a large circle of relations and friends.

Overwhelming as is this melancholy bereavement to his worthy family, in which he shone as a most affectionate husband and father, and benevolent master, there is still for them great consolation in knowing that he developed strong hopes of future bliss, that flourish above the tomb, immortal and unfading. Many of his latest moments were spent in prayer; and he maintained throughout this trying interval that propriety which belonged to the character of a man of sense, and that elevated dependence upon a higher power which became a Christian.

Such were, as we have been enabled to sketch them, the life and death of our deceased friend; we see pictured in them the employments of a man bent earnestly and steadily upon the faithful discharge of the duties which pertained to the situation allotted to him by his Creator. No meritorious artifice to attract the popular applause, no disingenuous manoeuvering, were perceptible in his character. These qualities rendered him firm and steady in his friendships. His loss will long be felt by the circle of relations whom he has left behind him; and his memory, as a soldier and a man, will be long and affectionately cherished by all to whom he was known.

How often, at the peaceful fireside of this revolutionary soldier, have we heard the tale of the deeds of others years! Even now, can we see, in fancy's eye, the grey-haired sire, traveling with increased emotion through the memorable battles of Gilford, Brandywine, Savannah and Eutaw Springs. His aged and failing eyes glisten again with the fire of youth! At the recollection of their resplendent glories, he springs forward from the venerable chair of age, and in the warmth of emotion, almost forgets, for the time, the lapse of years! But he is gone to the cold and silent tomb, mouldering into dust, and mingling again with his mother earth. No more shall his spirit rejoice in the cannon's roar, or the music of the drum. Triana, Madison Co., Ala., Aug. 28, 1832.—*Southern Advocate,* Huntsville, Sept. 8, 1832.

Mrs. P. H. Mell has collected some additional details, and her sketch is given in full, although it contains some repetitions:

"James Collier, a Revolutionary soldier, is buried on his plantation near Triana, Madison county, Alabama, about twenty miles from Huntsville.

"His wife is buried beside him and their monuments, with inscriptions, are now standing in a full state of preservation in the old family burying ground. The inscriptions are as follows:

" 'To the memory of
JAMES COLLIER,
who was born in Lunenburg Co., Va., Oct. 13th, A. D. 1757, and died the 20th of August, A. D. 1832.

" 'And though after my skin worms destroy this body, yet in my flesh shall I see God: whom I shall see for myself and my eyes shall behold and not another.' "

To the memory of
ELIZABETH BOULDIN,
of Charlotte Co., Va., wife of James Collier, who was born the 13th of Feb., A. D. 1763, and died the 23d of Feb., A. D. 1828.

" 'All flesh is grass, and all the goodliness thereof is as a flower of the field, for the wind passeth over it and it is gone and the place thereof shall know it no more.' "

"James Collier was the son of Cornelius Collier and Elizabeth Wyatt, of Lunenburg county, Va. He was descended from Charles Collier, of King and Queen county, Va., on his father's side, and his mother was nearly related to Sir Francis Wyatt, Colonial Governor of Virginia. It was the old flax wheel of his (James Collier's) cousin, Mary Collier, the ancestor of the late Prof. G. Brown Goode, which suggested the insignia of the Daughters of the American Revolution. James Collier was wounded at the battle of Eutaw Springs by a sabre cut across his cheek, in a hand-to-hand encounter with a British soldier. He killed the soldier and carried the scar on his face to his grave. His brother, Wyatt Collier, was killed in the same battle when only a boy.

"James Collier married Elizabeth Bouldin, July 3, 1788, daughter of James Bouldin and Sally Watkins, of Charlotte county, Va. He was a large land owner in Lunenburg county and resided there until 1802, when he, with his little family, followed his father and other relatives to Abbeville District, South Carolina. He was a large planter in that State until 1818, when he followed his sons to the territory of Alabama, his older sons having settled in that part of the Mississippi territory, now Alabama, in 1812. He settled on a large plantation in Madison county, where he lived and died.

"His wife, Elizabeth Bouldin, was the daughter of James Bouldin, who was the oldest son of Colonel Thomas Bouldin of Colonial fame, who settled in Lunenburg (now Charlotte) county, Virginia, in 1744, coming from Pennsylvania. His wife was Nancy Clark, niece of Captain Richard Wood of the English navy. The family of Bouldins are noted for their intellect and their love for the legal profession. Virginia boasts there has never been a generation without a judge, even to the present day. This couple left a large family of sons, but there were only four grandsons among the grandchildren. Governor Henry Watkins Collier was a son of James Collier. He was closely connected with the politics of Alabama from 1822 until his death in 1855.

"The ancestry of James Collier is as follows:
(1) Charles Collier of King and Queen county, Virginia. One of his children,—
(2) John Collier, Sr., (1680-1735), who was married three times, by his third wife, Nancy Eyres, had issue, among others:
(3) Cornelius Collier, born 1725, married Elizabeth Wyatt in Gloucester county, Va., about 1750, lived in Lunenburg coutny, Va., was a soldier in the Revolution and moved to Abbeville District, South Carolina in 1788; he had four sons and one of them was—
(4) James Collier, the subject of this sketch.
The facts of this article were furnished by his great-granddaughter, Miss Elizabeth R. Benagh. James Collier is mentioned in the *Memorial Record of Alabama*, vol. ii, p. 415."—*Transactions* of the Alabama Historical Society, Vol. iv, pp. 536-7.

COLLINS, ELISHA, aged 75, and a resident of Greene county; private Virginia Militia; enrolled on December 18, 1833, under act of Congress of June 7, 1832, payment to date from March 4, 1831; annual allowance, $30; sums received to date of publication of list, $90.—*Revolutionary Pension Roll*, in Vol. xiv, Sen. Doc. 514, 23rd Cong., 1st sess., 1833-34.

COLLINS, ELY, aged 76, and a resident of Limestone county; private N. C. Militia; enrolled on February 23, 1834, under act of Congress of June 7, 1832, payment to date from March 4, 1831; annual allowance, $40; sums received to date of publication of list, $100.—*Revolutionary Pension Roll,* in Vol. xiv, Sen. Doc., 514, 23rd Cong., 1st sess., 1833-34.

COOK, BENJAMIN, aged 82, resided in Monroe county, June 1, 1840.—*Census of Pensioners,* 1841, p. 149.

COOK, REUBEN, aged 74, and a resident of Fayette county; private N. C. Militia; enrolled on November 15, 1833, under act of Congress of June 7, 1832, payment to date from March 4, 1831; annual allowance, $36.66; sums received to date of publication of list, $109.98.—*Revolutionary Pension Roll,* in Vol. xiv, Sen. Doc. 514, 23rd Cong., 1st sess., 1833-34. He resided in Fayette county, June 1, 1840, aged 80.—*Census of Pensioners,* 1841, p. 148.

CORLEY, ZACCHEUS, aged 72, and a resident of Bibb county; private S. Carolina Militia; enrolled on March 8, 1834, under act of Congress of June 7, 1832, payment to date from March 4, 1831; annual allowance, $40; sums received to date of publication of list, $100.—*Revolutionary Pension Roll,* in Part 3, Vol. xiii, Sen. Doc. 514, 23rd Cong., 1st sess., 1833-34. He resided in Bibb county, June 1, 1840, aged 77.—*Census of Pensioners,* 1841, p. 149.

CORY, THOMAS, age not given, a resident of Mobile county; sergeant 4th Battalion Corps Artillery; enrolled on May 21, 1821, payment to date from February 15, 1821; annual allowance, $32; sums received to date of publication of list, $161.47; Acts Military establishment.—*Revolutionary Pension Roll,* in Vol. xiv, Sen. Doc. 514, 23rd Cong., 1st sess., 1833-34.

COTTON, JAMES, aged 69, and a resident of Madison county; private Virginia Militia; enrolled on March 2, 1833, under act of Congress of June 7, 1832, payment to date from March 4, 1831; annual allowance, $55; sums received to date of publication of list, $165.—*Revolutionary Pension Roll,* in Vol. xiv, Sen. Doc. 514, 23rd Cong., 1st sess., 1833-34.

COUCH, ELY, age not given, a resident of Russell county; corporal 4th Regular U. S. Infantry; enrolled on September 20, 1832, payment to date from August 1, 1832; annual allowance, $96; sums received to date of publication of list, $201.06; Acts Military establishment.—*Revolutionary Pension Roll,* in Vol. xiv, Sen. Doc. 514, 23rd Cong., 1st sess., 1833-34.

COURSON, JAMES, aged 72, and a resident of Montgomery county; private S. C. Continental Line and Militia;

Revolutionary Soldiers in Alabama.

enrolled on January 19, 1833, under act of Congress of June 7, 1832; payment to date from March 1831; annual allowance, $80; sums received to date of publication of list, $240.—*Revolutionary Pension Roll,* in Vol. xiv, Sen. Doc. 514, 23rd Cong., 1st sess., 1833-34.

COZBY, ROBERT, age not given, a resident of Lowndes county; private Revolutionary Army; enrolled on May 15, 1821; payment to date from February 14, 1821; annual allowance, $96; sums received to date of publication of list, $245.06; Acts Military establishment.—*Revolutionary Pension Roll,* in Vol. xiv, Sen. Doc. 514, 23rd Cong., 1st sess., 1833-34.

CRAFT, EZEKIEL, aged 72, and a resident of Madison county; private, dragoon and drummer S. C. Continental Line and Militia; enrolled on December 31, 1832, under act of Congress of June 7, 1832, payment to date from March 4, 1831; annual alowance, $93.33; sums received to date of publication of list, $279.99.—*Revolutionary Pension Roll,* in Vol. xiv, Sen. Doc. 514, 23rd Cong., 1st sess., 1833-34. He resided in Madison county, June 1, 1840, aged 77.—*Census of Pensioners,* 1841, p. 148.

CRAIG, JOHN, aged 71, and a resident of Limestone county; private Virginia Militia; enrolled on January 24, 1833, under act of Congress of June 7, 1832, payment to date from March 4, 1831; annual allowance, $28.34.—*Revolutionary Pension Roll,* in Vol. xiv, Sen. Doc. 514, 23rd Cong., 1st sess., 1833-34.

CRAIG, JOHN, aged 75, resided in Limestone county, June 1, 1840.—*Census of Pensioners,* p. 148.

CRANE, MAYFIELD, aged 67, and a resident of Pickens county; private S. C. State Troops; enrolled on April 13, 1834, under act of Congress of June 7, 1832, payment to date from March 4, 1831; annual allowance, $80.—*Revolutionary Pension Roll,* in Vol. xiv, Sen. Doc. 514, 23rd Cong., 1st sess., 1833-34.

CUNNINGHAM, ROBERT, aged 73, and a resident of Tuscaloosa county; private and sergeant, N. C. Continental Line and Militia; enrolled on June 5, 1833, under act of Congress of June 7, 1832, payment to date from March 4, 1871; annual allowance, $91.67; sums received to date of publication of list, $275.01.—*Revolutionary Pension Roll,* in Vol. xiv, Sen. Doc. 514, 23rd Cong., 1st sess., 1833-34.

Mrs. P. H. Mell in *Transactions* of the Alabama Historical Society, Vol. iv, pp. 537-541 has a full account of the life and services of this patriot.

"Rev. Robert Cunningham lies buried near the central part of the old cemetery in Tuscaloosa. A stately marble shaft marks his grave; the epitaph which covers the four sides of the shaft is in Latin, showing among other things that he had been a soldier of the Revolution, and pastor of Presbyterian churches in Georgia and in Lexington, Kentucky.

"These inscriptions are as follows:

On the west face:

Hic Sepultus Jacet
Vir ille
ROBERTUS M. CUNNINGHAM, D. D.
Belli Revolutionis
Americanae miles fidelis.
etiamque
Crucis Domini Jesu Christi:

On the east face:

Ecclesiae Presb.
in Republica Georgiae
Pastor
Multos annos.
Et in urbe Lexingtonia
Rep. Kentuckiensis
Eundem honorem tulit.

On the south face:

Qui
De Religione, de Patria
Optime meritus:
Maximo suorum
et bonorum omnuim
Desiderio
Mortem obiit,
Die Jul. XI: Anno Domini:
MDCCCXXXIX:
Aetatis suae
LXXX.

On the north face:

Uxor dilectissima
Hoc monumentum
ponendum
Curavit.

Revolutionary Soldiers in Alabama. 27

"The facts concerning the life of this distinguished man are mostly taken from Sanders' *Early Settlers of Alabama*, p. 197. The author says that the importance of historical societies is shown from the fact that very little information could be obtained for this biography from any source until he wrote to the Presbyterian Historical Society of Philadelphia, when he promptly received a circumstantial account of the events of his life.

"Robert M. Cunningham, a son of Roger and Mary Cunningham, was born in York county, Pennsylvania, September 10, 1760. In 1775 his parents removed to North Carolina. Query 293 of the Historical and Genealogical Department of the *Montgomery* (Ala.) *Advertiser* states that 'Roger Cunningham and wife, ——— Sturgeon, removed from near Gettysburg, Pennsylvania, to Mecklenburg county, North Carolina, just previous to the Revolutionary war. They had six children,—Robert, William, James, Nelly, Mary and Margaret.' There is little room to doubt that this is the same family as that of the subject of this sketch, and that his mother's name was Mary Sturgeon.

"Robert served as a youthful soldier in the North Carolina contingent during the Revolutionary war, but it is not known to what regiment he was attached. At the close of the war he went to school to the Rev. Robert Finley, Mr. Robert McCulloch and the Rev. Joseph Alexander. In 1787, being 26 years of age, he entered the junior class in Dickinson College, Carlisle, Pa., and graduated in 1789.

"On leaving college he returned to his parents and taught school while he studied theology. He was licensed to preach by the First Presbytery of South Carolina in 1792. Here he married his first wife, Elizabeth, daughter of Charles and Mary Moore, of Spartanburg District. A sketch of the life of Charles Moore is given in J. B. Landrum's *History of Spartanburg*, p. 189. He was a brave and faithful old patriot. Elizabeth died November 3, 1794, leaving a daughter who died young.

"In the autumn of 1792 he went to Georgia and organized a church called Ebenezer, in Hancock county; he also preached at Bethany church. October 15, 1795, he married Betsy Ann, daughter of Joseph Parks, of Prince Edward county, Virginia, and by this marriage he had five sons, one of whom was the Rev. Joseph Cunningham, a minister of ability. October 14, 1805, he married as a third wife, Emily, daughter of Col. William Bird, of Warren county, Georgia, originally from Pennsylvania, who survived him. Hers was a family of distinction.—See Dubose's *Life of Yancey*. Three of her aunts on her father's side married signers of the Declaration of Independence, James Wilson and George Ross, of Pennsylvania, and George Read, of Delaware. Her sister, Caroline Bird, married Benjamin Cudworth Yancey, and was the mother of the great Southern orator, William Lowndes Yancey. Another sister, Louisa Bird, married Captain Robert Cunningham of 'Rosemont,' South Carolina, a gentleman of great wealth, liberality and high culture, and an officer in the war of 1812. Their daughter, Miss Ann Pamela Cunningham, was the founder of the Mt. Vernon Ladies' Memorial Association and was its first regent. Another sister married Jesse Beene, of Cahaba, a distinguished lawyer and politician. A brother, Will E. Bird, was county judge of Dallas county, Alabama, 1836. It is a singular coincidence that Emily Bird married Rev. Robert Cunningham, of Georgia, and another sister, Louisa Bird, married Capt. Robert Cunningham, of South Carolina. Rev. Robert Cunningham at the time of his marriage must have won much distinction in a ministerial and social respect. By this last marriage he had a son, Robert, a physician, who died in Sumter county, Alabama, and three daughter,—Mrs. Maltby, Mrs. Wilson and Louisa.

"In 1807 he removed to Lexington, Kentucky, and was installed pastor of the First Presbyterian church. This town was even then celebrated for its wealth and intellectual culture and this pulpit required a minister of learning and eloquence. He remained in Lexington until 1822, when he removed to Moulton, in North Alabama. He had been laboring as a minister for thirty years, and, requiring some relaxation, he bought a plantation but preached in Moulton and surrounding villages. In 1826 he bought a farm eleven miles from Tuscaloosa and removed there. He built up churches in Tuscaloosa and at Carthage; he also preached occasionally at Greensboro, where his son, Joseph, was pastor. For eight years he preached a free gospel at Tuscaloosa. He preached his last sermon in 1838. He received the degree of doctor of divinity from Franklin College, Georgia (now the University), in 1827. In 1836 he removed to Tuscaloosa, and he died there on the 11th of July, 1839, 80 years of age. Dr. Cunningham was a man of impressive appearance; his height was more than six feet and his form was well developed; his features were good with expressive eyes; he was a man of

Revolutionary Soldiers in Alabama.

learning, eloquence and power in preaching; a man of charity, beloved by Christians of all denominations, and his tenderness in preaching opened many hearts. The old saint was called in Alabama 'Father Cunningham'; and he is thus described in Nall's *Dead of the Synod of Alabama*: 'Very few men ever exhibited more of clear and sound intellect—of tender, melting pathos—and of bold and manly eloquence than did this patriarch of the church.' "

CUNNINGHAM, WILLIAM N., aged 93, resided in Benton county, June 1, 1840.—*Census of Pensioners,* 1841, p. 148.

CURRY, THOMAS, sergeant, particular service not shown; annual allowance, $31.82; not demanded after March, 1831.—*Pension Book,* State Branch Bank, Mobile.

DAILY, OWEN, aged 76, resided in Monroe county, June 1, 1840.—*Census of Pensioners,* 1841, p. 149.

DARBY, BENJAMIN, aged 86, and a resident of Clarke county; private S. C. Militia; enrolled on April 18, 1833, under act of Congress of June 7, 1832, payment to date from March 4, 1831; annual allowance, $38.32; sums received to date of publication of list, $95.80.—*Revolutionary Pension Roll,* in Vol. xiv, Sen. Doc. 514, 23rd Cong., 1st sess., 1833-34.

DARDEN, GEORGE, aged 71, and a resident of Tuscaloosa county; private Georgia Militia; enrolled on April 2, 1833, under act of Congress of June 7, 1832, payment to date from March 4, 1831; annual allowance, $27.77; sums received to date of publication of list, $83.31.—*Revolutionary Pension Roll,* in Vol. xiv, Sen. Doc. 514, 23rd Cong., 1st sess., 1833-34.

DAVIS, JOHN, aged 61, and a resident of Mobile county; private S. C. Continental Line; enrolled on September 29, 1819, under act of Congress of March 18, 1818, payment to date from February 15, 1819; annual allowance, $96; dropped under act May 1, 1820.—*Revolutionary Pension Roll,* in Vol. xiv, Sen. Doc. 514, 23rd Cong., 1st sess., 1833-34.

DAVIS, LEWIS C, aged 78, and a resident of Autauga county; private Virginia State Troops; enrolled on May 19, 1834, under act of Congress of June 7, 1832, payment to date from March 4, 1831; annual allowance, $80.00.—*Revolutionary Pension Roll,* in Part 3, Vol. xiii, Sen. Doc. 514, 23rd Cong., 1st sess., 1833-34.

DAVIS, SAMUEL, aged 78, and a resident of Madison county, private Virginia Militia; enrolled on January 24,

1833, under act of Congress of June 7, 1832, payment to date from March 4, 1831; annual allowance $26.66; sums received to date of publication of list, $66.65.—*Revolutionary Pension Roll.* in Vol. xiv, Sen. Doc. 514, 23rd Cong., 1st sess., 1833-34. He resided in Madison county, June 1, 1840, aged 85.—*Census of Pensioners,* 1841, p. 148.

DAVIS, THOMAS,, aged 71, and a resident of Madison county; private S. C. State Troops; enrolled on November 15, 1833, under act of Congress of June 7, 1832; payment to date from March 4, 1831; annual allowance, $30; sums received to date of publication of list, $90.—*Revolutionary Pension Roll,* in Vol. xiv, Sen. Doc. 514, 23rd Cong., 1st sess., 1833-34.

DAVIS, WILLIAM, aged 73, and a resident of Greene county; private of Cavalry N. C. State Troops; enrolled on March 15, 1833, under act of Congress of June 7, 1832, payment to date from March 4, 1831; annual allowance, $100; sums received to date of publication of list, $200.—*Revolutionary Pension Roll,* in Vol. xiv, Sen. Doc. 514, 23rd Cong., 1st sess., 1833-34.

DAY, WILLIAM, age not given, and a resident of Dallas county; private S. C. Militia; enrolled on March 8, 1833, under act of Congress of June 7, 1832, payment to date from March 4, 1831; annual allowance, $40; sums received to date of publication of list, $120.—*Revolutionary Pension Roll,* Vol. xiv, Sen. Doc. 514, 23rd Cong., 1st sess., 1833-34.

DEAN, RICHARD, aged 75, and a resident of Madison county; private S. C. Continental Line; enrolled on January 24, 1833, under act of Congress of June 7, 1832, payment to date from March 4, 1831; annual allowance, $80; sums received to date of publication of list, $240.—*Revolutionary Pension Roll,* in Vol. xiv, Sen. Doc. 514, 23rd Cong., 1st sess., 1833-34. He resided in Madison county, June 1, 1840, aged 81.—*Census of Pensioners,* 1841, p. 148.

DEANE, JOHN, Sen., aged 75, and a resident of Clarke county; sergeant of Artillery, Virginia Continental Line and State Troops; enrolled on February 6, 1833, under act of Congress of June 7, 1832, payment to date from March 4, 1831; annual allowance, $120; sums received to date of publication of list, $360.—*Revolutionary Pension Roll,* in Part 3, Vol. xiii, Sen. Doc. 514, 23rd Cong., 1st sess., 1833-34.

DEARMAN, THOMAS M., aged 94, resided in Sumter county, June 1, 1840.—*Census of Pensioners,* 1841, p. 149.

Revolutionary Soldiers in Alabama. 31

DICKSON, ABNER, age not given; a resident of Franklin county; private Tennessee Volunteers; enrolled on March 10, 1818, payment to date from May 4, 1815; annual allowance, $96; sums received to date of publication of list, $1,808; April 24, 1816. Transferred from Montgomery county, Tennessee, from March 4, 1827.—*Revolutionary Pension Roll,* in Vol. xiv, Sen. Doc. 514, 23rd Cong., 1st sess., 1833-34.

DODD, JESSE, aged 77, and a resident of Lawrence county; private N. C. Continental Line; enrolled on September 6, 1817, under act of Congress of March 18, 1818, payment to date from September 25, 1818; annual allowance, $96; sums received to date of publication of list, $1,124.72.—*Revolutionary Pension Roll,* in Vol. xiv, Sen. Doc. 514, 23rd Cong., 1st sess., 1833-34.

DOYLE, EDWARD, aged 76, and a resident of Blount county; private S. C. Militia; enrolled on July 31, 1833, under act of Congress of June 7, 1832, payment to date from March 4, 1831; annual allowance, $87.50.—*Revolutionary Pension Roll,* in Part 3, Vol. xiii, Sen. Doc. 514, 23rd Cong., 1st sess., 1833-34.

DUNCAN, JOHN, aged 83, resided in Jackson county, June 1, 1840, with Robert Duncan.—*Census of Pensioners,* 1841, p. 148.

DUNSMOOR, JAMES, aged 75, and a resident of Morgan county; private N. C. Militia; enrolled on November 15, 1833, under act of Congress of June 7, 1832, payment to date from March 4, 1831; annual allowance, $20.—*Revolutionary Pension Roll,* in Vol. xiv, Sen. Doc. 514, 23rd Cong., 1st sess., 1833-34.

EARLE, SAMUEL, aged 75, and a resident of Washington county; private Virginia Continental Line; enrolled on January 5, 1833, under act of Congress of June 7, 1832, payment to date from March 4, 1831; annual allowance, $80; sums received to date of publication of list, $200.—*Revolutionary Pension Roll,* in Vol. xiv, Sen. Doc. 514, 23rd Cong., 1st sess., 1833-34.

EDDINS, BENJAMIN. "The subject of this sketch was a native of Virginia, and moved to South Carolina, many years previous to the American Revolution. He settled with his family in the upper part of the State, near Cambridge, or 'Old Ninety-Six.' By industry, prudence and economy, he has accumulated a handsome property and was living in great comfort and independence, when the war of the Revolution commenced. The ease and comfort of a home, however, with all of the luxuries of wealth, were as nothing to Mr. Eddins, when compared with the cause in which he found his country struggling.

"After the glorious repulse of Sir Peter Parker and Henry Clinton in their attack upon Fort Moultrie, in 1776, the citizens of South Carolina were suffered to live in peace until the fall of Charleston in 1780. Immediately after this unfortunate event, the whole South fell under the military Government of Great Britain. The inhabitants, in almost every part of the country, had to seek protection from such a source. They preferred dying with the liberties of their country, rather than to survive only to witness her degradation and subjection. Among these gallant spirits, whose names deserve being held in everlasting remembrance, was Benjamin Eddins. He attached himself to a small band of patriots, who stood out in defiance of the Royal Government, in old Ninety-Six district. Whilst bravely fighting under the standard of liberty, borne by his patriot band he was captured, and sent a prisoner of war to the British station at Ninety-Six, then under the command of Col. Cruger.

"Shortly after the capture of and imprisonment of Mr. Eddins a scouting party of the Tories went to his home, and after appropriating everything movable which they could find, they demanded of Mrs. Eddins her hidden treasures of money, and other articles of value. Making a virtue of necessity, she yielded everything of the kind which she possessed. But the plunderers were not satisfied and insisted that all had not been given up, and thereupon proceeded to abuse her shamefully and mistreat Mrs. Eddins.

An officer was guilty of the dastardly brutality of inflicting upon her a wound with his sword, which she carried to her grave. They then set fire to the dwelling house and outhouses, and in a few minutes, the whole were wrapped in flames.

"The news of the destruction of the property, and the mistreatment of the family, was carried to Mr. Eddins, whilst immured in the prison vaults. He received the information with the philosophy and calm resignation of a christian and a patriot. The fruits of his labor and industry, during a well spent life, were gone; but they had been sacrificed by his unflinching devotion to his country, and this was consolation enough for a spirit like his.

"After remaining some time in prison, unnoticed and perhaps unthought of, by those in whose custody he was, it was his good fortune to receive a visit from Col. Cruger, the commander of the station. The object of this visit was, to employ Eddins as a pilot for the foraging parties of the British army. He had a great while been living in that part of the country, and was better acquainted with its locality than almost any other person. Hence, his services would have been a matter of considerable importance to the British army. In order to secure him in such service, Col. Cruger offered him his liberty and liberal wages. They were instantly rejected with scorn and indignation. A commission in the British army was then tendered him, with a promise of indemnity for the property which he had lost. These tempting offers were likewise spurned. Threats were now resorted to, and in reply to these, Eddins said, 'I am, sir, your prisoner, and consequently completely in your power. You may, if you see proper, inflict any cruelty your imagination can invent. If it suits your love of torture, you may hitch a horse to each of my limbs and tear my body into four pieces: *Or you can'—unfolding his naked bosom to the Colonel—'cut out my heart and drain it of its last drop of blood; but, sir, my services belong to my country, and you never can command them.*' The boldness and the patriotic devotion of this high and noble expression—an expression worthy of the most illustrious hero that ever lived—touched the heart of the British officer, who was an accomplished gentleman, and a generous soldier and feeling alive to all of the noble impulses of our nature. 'You infatuated rebel,' replied the Colonel, 'You possess too bold a spirit and too honest a heart to linger out your days in prison—you are at liberty to go where you please, and dispose of your services as you may see proper.'

"Mr. Eddins was immediatetly released, and soon after joined the American army under General Pickens, where he continued to serve till the end of the war. He lived to a good old age, and died in Alabama, not many years since. He witnessed his country enjoying that liberty and independence, for which he had fought so manfully in his younger days.

"The above was given by a revolutionary soldier, who was in prison with Mr. Eddins, when visited by Col. Cruger."—"Revolutionary Incidents, No. 14," by Benjamin F. Perry in the *Greenville Mountaineer*, Greenville, S. C., Saturday, May 16, 1835.

EDDINS, WILLIAM, aged 70, and a resident of Madison county; dragoon Virginia Militia; enrolled on August 12, 1833, under act of Congress of June 7, 1832, payment to date from March 4, 1831; annual allowance, $100; sums received to date of publication of list, $200.—*Revolutionary Pension Roll*, in Vol. xiv, Sen. Doc. 514, 23rd Cong., 1st sess. 1833-34.

The *Greenville Mountaineer*, Greenville, S. C., June 27, 1835, has an interesting sketch of the services of Mr. Eddins. It was written by Gov. Benjamin F. Perry, a distinguished lawyer and political leader of South Carolina, and who devoted much time to local antiquarian and historical studies. The sketch is given in full:

"For the Mountaineer.

"REVOLUTIONARY INCIDENTS. NO. 20. WILLIAMS EDDINS, SEN.

"In a previous number of these incidents, the writer gave a brief sketch of the life, character and services of BENJAMIN EDDINS, a brave and gallant old spirit of the Revolution, who said to Col. Cruger, whilst a prisoner of war in a British garrison, 'I scorn your threats—you may take my life, or inflict on my person any cruelty your imagination can suggest—*but my services belong to my country, and you can never command them.*' Never was there a nobler sentiment uttered by the mouth of man. The far-famed reply of General Charles Cotesworth Pinckney to the French Ministry—'*Millions for defense, but not a cent for tribute,*' does not surpass it.

"The object of the present number, is to give some account of the Revolutionary services of Williams Eddins, the worthy son of this fearless and disinterested old patriot, and endowed with all of his father's devotion to his country, united with the natural ardor and enthusiasm of youth. At the age of sixteen, before most boys have left the leading strings of their mother, he shouldered his rifle, and marched forth to meet the enemy of his country, ready to 'sink or swim, live or die,' with the cause which his youthful heart had espoused. Not long after he had entered the service of his country, he was captured by the enemy, and started with other prisoners to the British fort at Ninety-Six. His arms were taken from him, as a matter of course, and his horse appropriated by one of the guards. Whilst they were thus marching on to Cambridge, the soldier who had taken possession of Eddins' horse, stopped to take a little American whiskey which he had also captured, dismounted, and laid his musket against a tree. Eddins was likewise suffered to halt, whilst the other prisoners, among whom was his father, continued their march. It is often said, that one drink with a veteran in the school of Bacchus, begets a thirst for another, and so it happened with the British soldier on the present occasion. He drank and loitered until the guard had got some distance ahead of him, and in the meantime, became rather careless of horse, gun and prisoner. A drunken man is very much inclined to be *liberal* and unsuspecting, but the veteran of Mars, as well of Bacchus, did not for a moment apprehend an attempt at escape, from a lad of Eddins' age and apearance. He was, however, mistaken for once, and the young prisoner, watching his opportunity, seized hold of the soldier's musket, mountetd his own horse, and rode off rather too fleetly to be overtaken.

"In this manner, William Eddins made his escape from a long and loathsome confinement, which befel the other prisoners. He made direct for home, to inform his mother of the capture and imprisonment of his father. The night that he reached home, he took the precaution to hide his gun in an old hollow log, secure from the weather as well as the search of the Tories. He had not been long in bed with a younger brother, when the house received a visit from the Tories. William and his brother secreted themselves between the bed and the wall, but not so as to elude the search of the Tories. After rumaging and looking about for some time, they discovered the feet of the two boys, and were in the act of pulling William out by the heel, when his mother said to them,—'do let the children alone.' They inferred from this expression, and the appearance of the boys, covered up in part by the bed that they were much younger and smaller than they actually were. In a short time the Tories left, and as they were going off, William, who was ever ready for an adventure, no matter how hazardous, determined to get up, take his gun from the hollow log, and give them a shot as they were going around the swamp not far off. His mother and brother did all they could to dissuade him, but in vain. He did as he had determined, and made his escape in safety. What effect his fire had is not known.

"In a few days after this, William joined Gen. Pickens, and marched with him into the Cherokee nation. They came very near the Indian town, and sent a couple of spies to reconnoitre. They returned and reported that the town was deserted. William Eddins was one of these selected for this purpose. Gen. Pickens then ordered thirteen of his soldiers to go and burn the houses. They crossed a little river, which separated the army under Pickens from the Indian town, and were marching carelessly on the summit of the hill, on which the town stood, when they received a shot fire from the Indians. 'It appeared,' said one of the company, 'as if the point of the hill was a blaze of fire.' Two young men, who were some distance ahead of the others, fell from their horses. The detachment then retreated, and formed for the purpose of resisting until assistance could come from the opposite side of the river. The horses of the two young men who fell, ran to the river, and there remained. There was a constant firing kept up between the Indians and the Whites. In the midst of this firing, Eddins saw the young men who were wounded rise up, and remain in a sitting posture. He knew from that that they were not so badly wounded as it was supposed, and immediately requested permission of Capt. Maxwell to attempt their rescue from danger. The Captain pointed out to him the peril of the enterprise, but consented for him to go, if he saw proper to do so. Instantly he caught their horses, rode to where they were, and assisted them in mounting, which they were able to do. The three then made their escape to the little detachment, which was by this time reinforced by the greater part of Gen. Pickens' army. As they got on their horses, one of the young men received two balls through the back of his coat, but sustained no injury. The Indians were immediately routed, and the town laid in ashes.

"William Eddins continued with Gen. Pickens until the close of the war, and he was left pennyless, and so was his father. During the ravages of the Revolution he endured much of the suffering and hardships of the American Revolution. When the country was restored to peace, he commenced farming, and made a crop of tobacco, which the old man often tells, without a horse. He is yet living near Huntsville, Alabama, upwards of seventy years of age, and has been a Baptist preacher, more than forty years. With the same zeal, sincerity, and boldness, with which he served his country in his younger days has he served his God in his old age and riper manhood."—B. F. P.

EDWARDS, JOHN, aged 82, and a resident of Perry county; private N. C. Militia; enrolled on September 26, 1833, under act of Congress of June 7, 1832, payment to date from March 4, 1831; annual allowance, $75; sums received to date of publication of list, $225.—*Revolutionary Pension Roll*, in Vol. xiv, Sen. Doc. 514, 23rd Cong., 1st sess., 1833-34.

ELLETT, JARVIS, aged 75, resided in Lawrence county, June 1, 1840, with Jon. Wilson.—*Census of Pensioners,* 1841, p. 148.

ELLIDGE, ABRAHAM, aged 74, and a resident of Lawrence county; private S. C. Militia; enrolled on October 19, 1833, under act of Congress of June 7, 1832, payment to date from March 4, 1831, annual allowance, $30; sums received to date of publication of list, $90.—*Revolutionary Pension Roll,* in Vol. xiv, Sen. Doc. 514, 23rd Cong., 1st sess., 1833-34. He resided in Lawrence county, June 1, 1840, aged 80.—*Census of Pensioners,* 1841, p. 148.

ELLIOTT, JOHN, aged 79, and a resident of Morgan county; private N. C. Militia; enrolled on July 10, 1834, under act of Congress of June 7, 1832, payment to date from March 4, 1831; annual allowance, $80.—*Revolutionary Pension Roll,* in Vol. xiv, Sen. Doc. 514, 23rd Cong., 1st sess., 1833-34.

ELMORE, JOHN ARCHER. Elmore county was named in honor of Gen. Elmore. He was deservedly popular for his "candor, good sense and sociability."

He was buried in the old family burying ground at the old homestead, "Huntington," in Elmore county. The following inscription is upon his tombstone:

IN
Memory of
GEN. JOHN ARCHER ELMORE,
who was born in
Prince Edward County, Va.,
August the 21st, 1762,
and died in
Autauga County, Ala.,
April 24th, 1834,
aged 71 yrs. 8 mos. & 3 days.
He was a soldier of the Revolution
in the Virginia Line
and afterwards a member of the Legislature
of So. Ca., and a General in
the militia.
He was a member of the Legislature of
Alabama
and filled various other offices of Honor and Trust
in both States.
He was an affectionate husband,
a kind and indulgent father,

a humane master,
A devoted friend, and a
patriotic citizen.

"General John Archer Elmore was born in Prince Edward county, Virginia, Aug. 21, 1762, and died in Autauga county, Alabama, April 24, 1834. He entered the Revolutionary service, a mere lad, in Greene's command in the Virginia line; was with him in his tour through the Carolinas, and with him at the surrender at Yorktown. This is shown by the archives in Washington; O'Neal's *Bench and Bar of South Carolina,* vol. ii, pp. 85, 88, and Brewer's *Alabama,* p. 109. After the Revolution he settled in Laurens district, South Carolina, and resided there many years, during which time he was often a member of the legislature. He moved to Autauga county, Alabama, in 1819 and served one term in the house of representatives from this county.

His first wife was Miss Saxon, by whom he had two sons: Hon. Franklin H. Elmore, of South Carolina, who succeeded Mr. Calhoun in the United States senate, and Benjamin F. Elmore, treasurer of South Carolina. His second wife, Miss Ann Martin, was a member of the famous Martin family of South Carolina, and descended also from the Marshall family of Virginia, and from Lieutenant Nathaniel Terry, of Virginia. By this second marriage there were five sons and several daughters. One of the daughters married Gov. Benj. Fitzpatrick, another married Hon. Dixon H. Lewis of Lowndes; another married Dr. J. T. Hearne, of Lowndes, and she is still (1904) living in Montgomery. The sons were Hon. John A. Elmore, a distinguished lawyer in Montgomery; William A. Elmore, a lawyer in New Orleans since 1835, superintendent of the mint until the outbreak of the war, and who died in Philadelphia in 1891; Capt. Rush Elmore, who commanded a company in the Mexican war and was territorial judge of Kansas; Henry Elmore, who was probate judge of Macon county prior to the war, and who afterwards moved to Texas; Albert Elmore, of Montgomery, secretary of State in 1865 and collector of customs in Mobile under President Johnson."—Mrs. P. H. Mell in *Transactions,* of the Alabama Historical Society, Vol. iv, pp. 541-2.

ENGLAND, WILLIAM, a resident of Perry county and later of Dallas; private, particular serivce not shown; enrolled on March 16, 1835, under act of Congress of June 7, 1832, payment to date from March 4, 1831; annual allowance, $30.— *Pension Book,* State Branch Bank, Mobile.

Revolutionary Soldiers in Alabama. 39

EVANS, OWEN, aged 78, and a resident of Morgan county; corporal S. C. Continental Line; enrolled on September 17, 1825, under act of Congress of March 18, 1818; payment to date from November 4, 1825; annual allowance, $96; sums received to date of publication of list, $128.—*Revolutionary Pension Roll,* in Vol. xiv, Sen. Doc. 514, 23rd Cong., 1st sess. ,1833-34.

FABER, WILLIAM, private, particular service not shown; enrolled on December 27, 1836; annual allowance, $100; no record of any payment having been made.—*Pension Book,* State Branch Bank, Mobile.

FAIR, BARNABAS, aged 76, and a resident of Tuscaloosa county; private N. C. Militia; enrolled on October 7, 1833, under act of Congress of June 7, 1832, payment to date from March 4, 1831; annual allowance, $80.—*Revolutionary Pension Roll,* in Vol. xiv, Sen. Doc. 514, 23rd Cong., 1st sess., 1833-34.

FIELDS, BARTHOLOMEW, aged 79, resided in Dale county, June 1, 1840.—*Census of Pensioners,* 1841, p. 149.

FILES, ADAM J., aged 78, resided in Macon county, June 1, 1840.—*Census Pensioners,* 1841, p. 149.

FILES, JEREMIAH, aged 70, and a resident of Blount county; private S. C. Militia; enrolled on September 26, 1833, under act of Congress of June 7, 1832, payment to date from March 4, 1831; annual allowance, $80; sums received to date of publication of list, $240.—*Revolutionary Pension Roll,* in Part 3, Vol. xiii, Sen. Doc. 514, 23rd Cong., 1st sess., 1833-34. He resided in Blount county, June 1, 1840, aged 75.—*Census of Pensioners,* 1841, p. 148.

FITZGERALD, JOHN, age not given, a resident of Washington county; private 7th Regular U. S. Infantry; enrolled on September 27, 1818, payment to date from August 26, 1818; annual allowance, $96; sums received to date of publication of list, $1,058.63; Acts military establishment. Died.—*Revolutionary Pension Roll,* in Vol. xiv, Sen. Doc. 514, 23rd Cong., 1st sess., 1833-34.

FLEMING, SAMUEL, aged 75, and a resident of Autauga county; private Georgia Militia; enrolled on January 12, 1833, under Act of Congress June 7, 1832, payment to date from March 4, 1831; annual allowance, $40; sums received to date of publication of list, $120.—*Revolutionary Pension Roll*, in Part 3, Vol. xiii, Sen. Doc. 514, 23rd Cong., 1st sess., 1833-34.

FLEMING, SAMUEL, aged 85, resided in Montgomery county, June 1, 1840.—*Census of Pensioners*, 1841, p. 149.

FLETCHER, WILLIAM, aged 76, and a resident of Jackson county; captain N. C. Militia; enrolled on January 2, 1834, under act of Congress of June 7, 1832, payment to date from March 4, 1831; annual allowance, $420; sums received to date of publication of list, $1,260.—*Revolutionary Pension Roll*, in Vol. xiv, Sen. Doc. 514, 23rd Cong., 1st sess., 1833-34.

FLUKER, GEORGE, aged 74, and a resident of Wilcox county; private S. C. Militia; enrolled on February 11, 1834, under act of Congress of June 7, 1832, payment to date from March 4, 1831; annual allowance, $80.—*Revolutionary Pension Roll*, in Vol. xiv, Sen. Doc. 514, 23rd Cong., 1st sess., 1833-34.

FOWLER, JOHN, sen., aged 99, resided in Pike county, June 1, 1840.—*Census of Pensioners*, 1841, p. 149.

FRANKS, MARSHALL, a resident of Pickens county; private and sergeant, particular service not shown; enrolled on December 27, 1836, under act of Congress of June 7, 1832, payment to date from March 4, 1831; annual allowance, $60 —*Pension Book*, State Branch Bank, Mobile.

FRENCH, BENJAMIN. "DIED—Near Rodgersville on the 21st inst., Mr. *Benjamin French*, aged 84 years, an old faithful Revolutionary soldier."—*Southern Advocate*, Huntsville, April 2, 1847.

FROXIL, JACOB, aged 85, resided in DeKalb county, June 1, 1840.—*Census of Pensioners*, 1841, p. 148.

FULLER, LITTLETON, aged 74, and a resident of Tuscaloosa county; private S. C. Militia; enrolled on September 17, 1833, under act of Congress of June 7, 1832, payment to date from March 4, 1831; annual allowance, $30.—*Revolutionary Pension Roll*, in Vol. xiv, Sen. Doc. 514, 23rd Cong., 1st sess., 1833-34.

FULTON, THOMAS, aged 81, resided in Lawrence county, June 1, 1840.—*Census of Pensioners*, 1841, p. 148.

Revolutionary Soldiers in Alabama. 41

GALESPIE, DANIEL, aged 77, resided in Chambers county, June 1, 1840, with David Taylor.—*Census of Pensioners*, 1841, p. 149.

GARISON, STEPHEN, aged 83, resided in Walker county, June 1, 1840, with Silas Garison.—*Census of Pensioners*, 1841, p. 150.

GARNER, JOHN, age not given, a resident of Butler county; service not given because of the loss of papers by the burning of the office of the War Department, 1801 and 1814; enrolled on July 5, 1812; payment to date from January 29, 1812; annual allowance, $48; sums received to date of publication of list, $1,060.78; Acts Military establishment; transferred from Georgia from March 4, 1824.—*Revolutionary Pension Roll*, in Vol. xiv, Sen. Doc. 514, 23rd Cong., 1st sess., 1833-34. He resided in Wilcox county, June 1, 1840, with William H. Wait, aged 81.—*Census of Pensioners*, 1841, p. 149.

GARNER, JOS., Sen., aged 95, resided in Cherokee county, June 1, 1840.—*Census of Pensioners*, 1841, p. 148.

GARNER, JOSEPH, aged 78, and a resident of St. Clair county; private Virginia Continental Line; enrolled on June 7, 1819, under act of Congress of March 18, 1818, payment to date from June 26, 1818; annual allowance, $96; sums received to date of publication of list, $1,506.39; transferred from Clark county, Georgia, from March 4, 1820.—*Revolutionary Pension Roll*, in Vol. xiv, Sen. Doc. 514, 23rd Cong., 1st sess., 1833-34.

GARNER, STURDY, aged 72, and a resident of Madison county; private N. C. Militia; enrolled on April 23, 1833, under act of Congress of June 7, 1832, payment to date from March 4, 1831; annual allowance, $33.33; sums received to date of publication of list, $72.33.—*Revolutionary Pension Roll*, in Vol. xiv, Sen. Doc. 514, 23rd Cong., 1st sess., 1833-34. He resided in Madison county, June 1, 1840, aged 72.—*Census of Pensioners*, 1841, p. 148.

GARRARD, WILLIAM, aged 72, and a resident of Lauderdale county; private Virginia State Troops; enrolled on October 7, 1833, under act of Congress of June 7, 1832, payment to date from March 4, 1831; annual allowance, $60.—*Revolutionary Pension Roll*, in Vol. xiv, Sen. Doc. 514, 23rd Cong., 1st sess., 1833-34.

GARRISON, STEPHEN, a resident of Lawrence county; private Regular N. C. Line; enrolled on April 26, 1830, under act of Congress of May 15, 1828, payment to date from March 3, 1826; annual allowance, $80; sums received to date of publication of list, $680; P. W. Taylor, agent.—*Revolutionary Pension Roll,* in Vol. xiv, Sen. Doc. 514, 23rd Cong., 1st sess., 1833-34.

GASSAWAY, JAMES, a resident of Shelby county; private, particular service not shown; enrolled on May 17, 1819, under act of Congress of March 18, 1818; annual allowance, $96; transferred from South Carolina.—*Pension Book,* State Branch Bank, Mobile.

GASTON, HUGH, a resident of Wilcox county; private, particular service not shown; enrolled on April 7, 1836, under act of Congress of June 7, 1832, payment to date from March 4, 1831; annual allowance, $20.—*Pension Book,* State Branch Bank, Mobile.

GEESLIN, CHARLES (Geesling in the *Census* list), aged 90, and a resident of Tuscaloosa county; private N. C. Continental Line; enrolled on April 8, 1825, under act of Congress of March 18, 1818, payment to date from August 17, 1824; annual allowance, $96; sums received to date of publication of list, $916.93.—*Revolutionary Pension Roll,* in Vol. xiv, Sen. Doc. 514, 23rd Cong., 1st sess., 1833-34. He resided in Tuscaloosa county, June 1, 1840, aged 99.—*Census of Pensioners,* 1841, p. 149.

GILL, JAMES, aged 74, and a resident of Greene county; private S. C. Militia; enrolled on September 16, 1833, under act of Congress of June 7, 1832; payment to date from March 4, 1831; annual allowance, $80; sums received to date of publication of list, $240.—*Revolutionary Pension Roll,* in Vol. xiv, Sen. Doc. 514, 23rd Cong., 1st sess., 1833-34.

GILLESPIE, JAMES, private, particular service not shown; date of enrollment not given, payment dates from September 4, 1833; annual allowance, $80.—*Pension Book,* State Branch Bank, Mobile. He resided in Pickens county, with John O. Gillespie, aged 78 years, June 1, 1840.—*Census of Pensioners,* 1841, p. 149.

GILMORE, GEORGE, a resident of Montgomery county; private, particular service not shown; enrolled on March 22, 1837, under act of Congress of June 7, 1832, payment to date

Revolutionary Soldiers in Alabama. 43

from March 4, 1831; annual allowance, $20.—*Pension Book,* State Branch Bank, Mobile.

GILMORE, JOHN, a resident of Marengo county; private, particular service not shown; enrolled on April 26, 1836, under act of Congress of June 7, 1832, payment to date from March 4, 1831; annual allowance, $21.66.—*Pension Book,* State Branch Bank, Mobile. He resided in Marengo county, June 1, 1840, aged 81.—*Census of Pensioners,* 1841, p. 148.

GILPIN, BENJAMIN, a resident of Henry county; private in cavalry and infantry, particular service not shown; enrolled on March 30, 1838, under act of Congress of June 7, 1832, payment to date from March 4, 1831; annual allowance, $86.67.—*Pension Book,* State Branch Bank, Mobile.

GLAZE, THOMAS, aged 89, resided in Fayette county, June 1, 1840.—*Census of Pensioners,* 1841, p. 148.

GLOVER, BENJAMIN, aged 81, and a resident of Madison county; private Maryland Militia; enrolled on January 24, 1833, under act of Congress of June 7, 1832, payment to date from March 4, 1831; annual allowance, $46.66; sums received to date of publication of list, $139.98.—*Revolutionary Pension Roll,* in Vol. xiv, Sen. Doc. 514, 23rd Cong., 1st sess., 1833-34.

GOGGANS, ALEXANDER. Alexander Goggans, a soldier of the Revolution, was born in Richmond county, Va., January 14, 1758. In early life, his parents emigrated to Newberry District, South Carolina. Young Goggans was an active soldier in the Revolutionary service. He was in Col. Williams' command at the battle of King's Mountain, where he was wounded in the left shoulder. Sometime afterwards while with a scouting party he was wounded in the left leg. And again, in another skirmish, he was struck down by a severe sabre stroke on the head and left for dead upon the field. After his recovery from this third wound, he rejoined his comrades and continued an active partisan to the end of the war. After peace was made, Mr. Goggans married Mary Dashields, who died in 1800. About 1815, he married Elizabeth Kilpatrick. After many years' residence in South Carolina, Mr. Goggans emigrated to Lincoln county, Tennessee. Thence in 1819 he emigrated to Lawrence county, Alabama, where he resided until the death of his wife in 1836. He then moved to Carroll county, Georgia, where he died March 21, 1852, in the triumphs of a living Faith. He was buried the next day with military honors in the graveyard at Bethany church.—Condensed from a sketch in *Jacksonville Republican,* Jacksonville, Ala., June 8, 1852.

GOODE, THOMAS, aged 74, and a resident of Jefferson county; private Virginia Continental Line; enrolled on September 22, 1819, under act of Congress of March 18, 1818, payment to date from April 15, 1818; annual allowance, $96; sums received to date of publication of list, $896.70; transferred from Christian county, Kentucky, from March 23, 1826.—*Revolutionary Pension Roll,* in Vol. xiv, Sen. Doc. 514, 23rd Cong., 1st sess., 1833-34.

GOODWIN, THEOPHILUS, aged 74, and a resident of Butler county; private N. C. Continental Line; enrolled on September 18, 1818, under act of Congress of March 18, 1818; payment to date from June 5, 1818; annual allowance, $96; sums received to date of publication of list, $1,511.46; transferred from Edgefield district, S. C., from *September 4, 1828.—*Revolutionary Pension Roll,* in Vol. xiv, Sen. Doc. 514, 23rd Cong., 1st sess., 1833-34. Also resided in Bibb county.—*Pension Book,* State Branch Bank, Mobile.

GRAGG, HENRY, a resident of Shelby county; private, particular service not shown; enrolled on April 26, 1836, under act of Congress of June 7, 1832, payment to date from March 4, 1831; annual allowance, $30.—*Pension Book,* State Branch Bank, Mobile. He resided in Shelby county, June 1, 1840, aged 79.—*Census of Pensioners,* 1841, p. 149.

GRAHAM, ANDREW, aged 78, and a resident of Franklin county; private S. C .Militia; enrolled on January 30, 1833, under act of Congress of June 7, 1832, payment to date from March 4, 1831; annual allowance, $33.66; sums received to date of publication of list, $84.15.—*Revolutionary Pension Roll,* in Vol. xiv, Sen. Doc. 514, 23rd Cong., 1st sess., 1833-34.

GRANT, JEREMIAH, age not given, a resident of Tuscaloosa county; private 6th Regular U. S. Infantry; enrolled on July 12, 1822, payment to date from April 12, 1820; annual allowance. $96; Acts Military establishment.—*Revolutionary Pension Roll,* in Vol. xiv, Sen. Doc. 514, 23rd Cong., 1st sess., 1833-34.

GREER, MOSES, aged 75, and a resident of Autauga county; private Georgia Militia; enrolled on August 12, 1833, under act of Congress of June 7, 1832, payment to date from

Revolutionary Soldiers in Alabama. 45

March 4, 1831; annual allowance, $28; sums received to date of publication of list, $84.—*Revolutionary Pension Roll,* in Part 3, Vol. xiii, Sen. Doc. 514, 23rd Cong., 1st sess., 1833-34.

GREESHAM (sic), ROBERT, age not given, a resident of Limestone county; private Dark's Regiment; enrolled on December 6 ,1824; payment to date from February 18, 1824; annual allowance, $48; sums received to date of publication of list, $433.95; February 4, 1822.—*Revolutionary Pension Roll,* in Vol. xiv, Sen. Doc. 514, 23rd Cong., 1st sess., 1833-34.

GREGG, SAMUEL, aged 77, and a resident of Lawrence county; private Virginia Militia; enrolled on April 23, 1833, under act of Congress of June 7, 1832, payment to date from March 4, 1831; annual allowance, $33.33; sums received to date of publication of list, $99.99.—*Revolutionary Pension Roll,* in Vol. xiv, Sen. Doc. 514, 23rd Cong., 1st sess., 1833-34.

GREWER, JOHN, aged 42, resided in Cherokee county, June 1, 1840.—*Census of Pensioners,* 1841, p. 148.

GRIFFIN, JOHN, aged 97, resided in Pike county, June 1, 1840.—*Census of Pensioners,* 1841, p. 149.

GUESS, BENJAMIN, aged 77, and a resident of Fayette county; private N. C. Militia; enrolled on June 16, 1833, under act of Congress of June 7, 1832, payment to date from March 4, 1831; annual allowance, $66.66.—*Revolutionary Pension Roll,* in Vol. xiv, Sen. Doc. 514, 23rd Cong., 1st sess., 1833-34. He resided in Fayette county, June 1, 1840, with Jesse Howard, aged 83.—*Census of Pensioners,* 1841, p. 148.

GURLEY, JEREMIAH, aged 75, and a resident of Madison county; private N. C. State Troops; enrolled on October 7, 1833, under act of Congress of June 7, 1832, payment to date from March 4, 1831; annual allowance, $57.08; sums received to date of publication of list, $171.24.—*Revolutionary Pension Roll,* in Vol. xiv, Sen. Doc. 514, 23rd Cong., 1st sess., 1833-34. He resided in Madison county, June 1, 1840, with John Gurley, aged 81.—*Census of Pensioners,* 1841, p. 148.

HAGGARD, HENRY, aged 94, resided in Bibb county, June 1, 1840, with James Fancher.—*Census of Pensioners,* 1841, p. 149.

HAGUE, JOHN. From the *South Western Christian Advocate,* published at Nashville, July 24, 1841.

" 'AN OLD SOLDIER FALLEN.—Mr. John Hague, aged, (we understand) ninety-three years, died in Nashville, on the 13th inst. Mr. Hague was a native of Germany. He came to America in company with Lafayette, and fought in the Revolutionary War in aid of our country's independence. He was one of Lafayette's light guard. When this distinguished chieftain visited America, and passed through Nashville in 1824, Mr. Hague, who then resided in Huntsville, Alabama, came on foot, more than a hundred miles, to meet once more his old General. We are told by those who were present at their meeting, that it was a moment of thrilling interest. Mr. Hague threw himself suddenly and unexpectedly before Lafayette; the General immediately recognized him, and with a familiar tone exclaimed ,'Why, John, is this you!' and in a moment they were closely embraced in each other's arms.

" 'Mr. Hague was for more than fifty years a devoted Christian, and faithful member of the Methodist Episcopal church.

" 'He died triumphantly. His funeral was attended by an immense concourse. He was buried with military honors.' "—*Independent Monitor*, Tuscumbia, Aug. 11, 1841.

The following further reference to this old soldier is noted, evidently taken from some Nashville paper:

"During the visit, short as it was, of Gen. Lafayette to this place [Nashville], many incidents occurred, calculated to touch the feelings and awaken the sensibility of all who witnessed them. From among the number which have been described to us, we select the following:

"An old 'revolutionaire' named Hagy, a German by birth, who came to America in the same vessel with Gen. Lafayette, in 1777, and served with him during the greater part of the war, had travelled hither on foot from Huntsville to greet the 'Nation's Guest.' Their meeting under our civic arch was most cordial. Hagy repeatedly embraced and kissed his old commander."—*Southern Advocate*, Huntsville, Ala., May 27, 1825.

HALL, WILLIAM, aged 84, and a resident of St. Clair county; private S. C. Militia; enrolled on July 20, 1833, under act of Congress of June 7, 1832, payment to date from March 4, 1831; annual allowance, $36.34; sums received to date of publication of list, $90.85.—*Revolutionary Pension Roll*, in Vol. xiv, Sen. Doc. 514, 23rd Cong., 1st sess., 1833-34.

HAMILTON, THOMAS. "Thomas Hamilton, one of the five children of David Hamilton and Margaret Carlisle, was born in Belfast, Ireland, April 9, 1758. Their family emigrated to America about 1762, landing in Virginia after a voyage of nearly three months. Upon their arrival, David Hamilton settled in Culpepper county, where he lived with one of his sons. Thomas Hamilton was married on the 28th of May, 1782, to Temperance Arnold, daughter of Benjamin Arnold and Ann Hendrick of South Carolina During the Revolution, Benjamin Arnold, an old man, left South Carolina on account of the troubles resulting from the war, and carried his family for greater safety to Culpepper county, Va., where they became acquainted with Thomas Hamilton. After their marriage in 1782, they returned to the old home of Benjamin Arnold in South Carolina, where they settled upon a place between Andy creek on the east and Horse creek on the west in Greenville district. Here they lived until 1821, when they moved to Butler county, Ala., near Greenville, and remained there until 1826, when they moved to Lowndes county, ten miles south of Benton, where they both died. They are buried in Watkins cemetery, near Collirene, Lowndes county. Thomas died in August, 1844, aged 86, and his wife July 22, 1849, aged 87. The spot is marked by a marble obelisk, erected to the memory of the family. The following inscription, with no dates, is among others: 'Thomas and Temperance Hamilton rest here.' Thomas Hamilton was with Sumter but not in the regular army. He was at the battles of the Cowpens, Eutaw Springs and King's Mountain. He was in the brigade commanded by Colonel Campbell at the latter place. After his death in 1844, over sixty years after the Revolutionary war, few of the participants of that mighty struggle were left on earth. The citizens of Lowndes county asked permission to bury him with military honors." At the age of 81 he resided in Lowndes county, June 1, 1840.—*Census of Pensioners*, 1841, p. 149.—Mrs. P. H. Mell in the *Tranactions* of the Alabama Historical Society, Vol. iv, p. 542.

HAMMAN, PHIL. On Saturday, July 3, 1830, the fifty-fifth anniversary of American independence was celebrated at Bellefonte, Jackson county, Alabama, at which among other participants were several Revolutionary patriots. After the reading of the Declaration of Independence by Henry F. Scruggs and the delivery of an oration by Hon. Samuel Moore, the company sat down to a plentiful dinner. After this many patriotic toasts were drunk. Only one, and that because of the historic fact it evoked, is here reproduced:

"*By L. James, Esq.* 'Capt. Phil Hamman: The Saviour of Greenbrier—tho' his history is but little known, his intrepidity and patriotism are not less worthy of our commendation.'

"After the drinking of this toast, the old soldier rose and said: He thanked the gentlemen for introducing his name on an occasion where he had already been too much honored. Tho' his history was not much known, he could not object to have the transactions of his life divulged to the world. For nine years he had been in the wars of his country—during a greater part of which he had been engaged in the most dangerous parts of Indian service. He had suffered much; on one occasion he had been stripped by savage rapacity of every vestige of property he possessed, even the clothing of himself and family—one of his children fell a victim to their cruelty. But not to dwell on the dangers he had endured, he would merely speak of the occasion so kindly alluded to in the toast. When stationed at Fort Randolph, at the mouth of the Big Kanawha, nine hundred Indians set off in a body to make an unexpected attack on the inhabitants of Greenbrier, Virginia. Two men were despatched to apprize the people in that quarter of their approaching danger. In three days they returned, wounded, and in despair; others were sought for who would carry the express; none were found willing to engage in so dangerous and hopeless an undertaking—when he and one John Pryor (who was afterwards killed by the Indians) painted and dressed in Indian garb, set off, and in forty-eight hours travelled one hundred and sixty miles through the wilderness: they overtook the Indians within twelve miles of the white settlements, passed through their camps, and gave timely warning to the people of their impending danger.—Such preparations were made for security and defense as the occasion permitted. About daylight a violent attack was made on Fort Donley; the conflict was desperate—the door of the Fort was broken open—he stood in it, and resisted the enemy—'till it could be shut and fastened. The foe were repelled with great loss, and the country saved from savage barbarity. He said that although he was old and poor, and had not received the compensation promised him by his country, yet he thanked God he was in peace and safety, and could live 'without the aid of public or private charity.' He then offered the following sentiment:

"'OUR RULERS: May they be just men, fearing God, and hating covetousness.'"—*Southern Advocate*, Huntsville, July 10, 1830.

Revolutionary Soldiers in Alabama. 49

HAMMOND, SAMUEL, aged 88, resided in Sumter county, June 1, 1840.—*Census of Pensioners*, 1841, p. 149.

HANCOCK, ROBERT. "Died—At his residence, ten miles northwest from Huntsville, on the 15th inst., The Rev. ROBERT HANCOCK, in the 77th year of his age. He was a native of Nottoway county, Virginia. In the year 1790, he emigrated to South Carolina, and from thence in 1811, to his late residence in this county. Mr. Hancock was amiable in his disposition, industrious in his habits, and thereby rendered his family both easy, and happy in their circumstances. He was a true patriot, and during the great revolutionary struggle felt much interest for the safety and welfare of his country, and though disabled by an unavoidable accident to render actual service, he did everything in the compass of his power to promote the cause of liberty. But above all, he was a true friend to religion, and a sincere lover of his God; for 52 years he has been an acceptable member of the Methodist Episcopal church, and for about 30 years a local minister of said church. His talents were respectable, his piety deep, his zeal ardent, his conduct irreproachable, his usefulness extensive; in short, he was a light in a benighted land, and like unto a city set on a hill which cannot be hid,—and now, though he is dead, he will be remembered as one of the church's brightest ornaments for more than a half a century. His memory will ever be cherished with the fondest recollections by his surviving children, friends, and numerous acquaintances. But he has gone to the house appointed for all the living, yet our loss is his infinite gain; he is not dead, but is only sleeping in Jesus. Such will God bring with Him, therefore we sorrow not as those who have no hope. His last illness was long, and his afflictions severe, yet he evinced the patience and fortitude of a christian soldier; and notwithstanding his body was worn down by old age and infirmity, his mind in a great degree retained vigor until the last; and with the prospect of eternal life full in view, he calmly sank in the arms of his blessed Jesus. 'Mark the perfect man, and behold the upright, for the end of that man is *peace*.' 'Let me die the death of the righteous, and let my last end be like his.'"—*Communicated.—The Democrat*, Huntsville, Ala., April 21, 1831.

HARDIN, JOSEPH, aged 74, and a resident of Tuscaloosa county; private N. C. Militia; enrolled on October 29, 1833, under act of Congress of June 7, 1832, payment to date from March 4, 1831; annual allowance, $26.66; sums received to date of publication of list, $79.98.—*Rveolutionary Pension Roll,* in Vol. xiv, Sen. Doc. 514, 23rd Cong., 1st sess., 1833-34.

HARGRAVE, WILLIAM, aged 75, and a resident of Marengo county; ensign N. C. Continental Line; enrolled on January 25, 1818, under act of Congress of March 18, 1818, payment to date from June 15, 1818; annual allowance, $240; sums received to date of publication of list, $501.32.—*Revolutionary Pension Roll,* in Vol. xiv, Sen. Doc. 514, 23rd Cong., 1st sess., 1833-34.

HARPER, THOMAS, aged 76 and a resident of Pickens county; private Pennsylvania Continental Line; enrolled on July 30, 1834, under act of Congress of June 7, 1832, payment to date from March 4, 1831; annual allowance, $20.—*Revolutionary Pension Roll,* in Vol. xiv, Sen. Doc. 514, 23rd Cong., 1st sess., 1833-34.

HARRIS, HENRY, aged 76, and a resident of Madison county; private Virginia Continental Line; enrolled on March 17, 1819, under act of Congress of March 18, 1818, payment to date from May 22, 1818; annual allowance, $96; sums received to date of publication of list, $1,467.64; transferred from Frederick county, Virginia, from September 4, 1823.—*Revolutionary Pension Roll,* in Vol. xiv, Sen. Doc. 514, 23rd Cong., 1st sess., 1833-34. The following interesting sketch will give further personal details:

[*From the Star-Spangled Banner of Oct. 24th.*]

"ANOTHER REVOLUTIONARY WORTHY GONE!

"Departed this life on the evening of the 22d instant, at the residence of his son in this place, Mr. HENRY HARRIS, in the 75th year of his age. Mr. HARRIS was a native of Richmond county, Va., and at a very early period of the Revolution enlisted at Fredericksburg (Va.) in Col. Baylor's Regiment of Dragoons. From the time of his enlistment until the close of the war, he was actively engaged in the service of his country. In most of the important battles that were fought, he bore his share. He was present at the surrender of Burgoyne—at the battles of the Brandywine, the Cowpens, Camden, Gilford and Yorktown. From the time of his retirement from the army until his death, he had lived in the Western and Southwestern States; and throughout a long life sustained the reputation acquired in early youth. It was his glory to think that he had aided in freeing his country from oppression, and it was his fondest boast that he had served under the eye of his great commander WASHINGTON. When stretched upon the bed of weakness and old age he viewed his approaching end with the calmness and fortitude which characterized him when struggling in the deadly combat with the enemies of his country. For some time previous to his death, his mind seemed to dwell upon the incidents of his early life—and it was truly affecting to listen to the old man, and hear him accounting the battles of his youth,

"Shoulder the crutch and show how fields were won.

"It was his dying request that he should be buried with military honors; and accordingly when it was announced that he had ceased to live, the 'HUNTSVILLE GUARDS' proceeded to make arrangements for his interment. On yesterday at half past 10, the Guards reached his late residence, and as the procession moved from the house, the ARTILLERY COMPANY under the direction of their public spirited commander CAPT. LYNES commenced firing minute guns. Thirteen rounds were fired by the time the procession reached the graveyard: here the usual military obsequies were performed by the Guards.

"Here we might pause; for surely it is enough to secure the regret of every American, by simply announcing that the deceased was a soldier of the Revolution; but justice to his memory requires of us to say, that as a man, he lived respected and died lamented by all who knew him."—*Southern Advocate,* Huntsville, Oct. 29, 1833.

HARRIS, RICHARD, aged 75, and a resident of Madison county; private Massachusetts Militia; enrolled on Sepetmber 26, 1833, under act of Congress of June 7, 1832, payment to date from March 4, 1831; annual allowance, $80; sums received to date of publication of list, $200.—*Revolutionary Pension Roll,* in Vol. xiv, Sen. Doc. 514, 23rd Cong., 1st sess., 1833-34. He resided in Madison county, June 1, 1840.—*Census of Pensioners,* 1841, p. 148.

"ANOTHER REVOLUTIONARY SOLDIER GONE.

"Died, in Madison county, Ala., January 23d, 1853, Capt. RICHARD HARRIS. The deceased was born in Powhatan county, Va., on the 20th November, 1758. When but a youth, at the age of 17, he entered the army, and with that veteran band of soldiers, fighting for liberty and truth, devoted himself to his country's interests till the close of the war. He was an eye-witness of the surrender of Lord Cornwallis at Little York. After having shared with his countrymen the hardships of war, he returned to his home and friends to enjoy that glorious boon, *liberty,* for which he had so earnestly contended.

"Soon after the war, he devoted himself to the service of God and the good of his fellow men. He professed religion in Powhatan county, Va., and soon after united himself with the M. E. church, where he remained, for more than half a century, a consistent, useful, and much loved member.—Hospitable, kind, generous, you had only to look upon his noble face to behold all those commanding and ennobling virtues which adorn human nature. He removed from Virginia to Madison county, Ala., in 1809, and resided near Blue Spring till the day of his death. We do not say he was without fault, but we do say that few men have lived as long as he did with as few censurers and with as few enemies. He closed his earthly warfare as he closed the revolutionary war, in triumph and glory. He has left many friends to mourn his loss."—*The Southern Advocate*, Huntsville, Feb. 9, 1853.

HART, HENRY, aged 71, and a resident of Greene county; private S. C. Militia; enrolled on September 26, 1833, under act of Congress of June 7, 1832, payment to date from March 4, 1831; annual allowance, $80; sums received to date of publication of list, $240.—*Revolutionary Pension Roll*, in Vol. xiv, Sen. Doc. 514, 23rd Cong., 1st sess., 1833-34. He resided in Greene county, June 1, 1840, aged 76.—*Census of Pensioners*, 1841, p. 149.

HARVEY, JOHN, aged 75, and a resident of Lawrence county; private N. C. State Troops; enrolled on March 1, 1833, under act of Congress of June 7, 1832, payment to date from March 4, 1831; annual allowance, $26.66.—*Revolutionary Pension Roll*, in Vol. xiv, Sen. Doc. 514, 23rd Cong., 1st sess., 1833-34. He resided in Lawrence county, June 1, 1840, aged 82.—*Census of Pensioners*, 1841, p. 148.

"DIED, in Lawrence county on the 23rd inst., Rev. JOHN HARVEY, an old Revolutionary veteran, in the 86th year of his age. These old soldiers are dropping into the grave rapidly, and there will soon be none of them left for Mr. Polk to vote against receiving pensions."—*Southern Advocate*, Huntsville, Nov. 1, 1844.

Dr. Anson West in his *History of Methodism in Alabama*, p. 219, has the following brief tribute:

"John Harvey, who afterward attained to elder's orders, and who continued a member of the Quarterly Conference of the Franklin Circuit until 1831, and who was a native of Virginian, and a Revolutionary soldier, and who was naturally endowed with the gifts of oratory, and was talented and pious,

Revolutionary Soldiers in Alabama. 53

had his membership at Kitty Casky at the time of the Quarterly Conference above mentioned, and he died at that place afterward."

HAUGHTON, ABRM., aged 81, resided in Lawrence county, June 1, 1840, with William Boyce.—*Census of Pensioners,* 1841, p. 148.

HEARNE, WILLIAM. In the *Memorial Record of Alabama,* vol. ii, p. 426, mention is made of William Hearne from North Carolina, a Revolutionary soldier, and it states that he died in Lowndes county, Ala. The grave is in a private burying ground which is now on the plantation belonging to I. D. Hauser of Opelika. It is on that part of the plantation that he bought of the Mickle estate, and very near Manack station. It is surrounded by a brick wall and apparently contains three or four graves.

William Hearne was a great-grandson of William Hearne of Maryland (1630), a wealthy merchant and planter. Thomas Hearne, a son of this colonist, married Sally Wingate; he had twelve children, one of them, Nehemiah, married Betty ——— and lived in Somerset county, Md. A son of Nehemiah, William Hearne, was born in Somerset county, Md., in 1746; he married his cousin, Tabitha Hearne, and moved to North Carolina, when it was a new country. At the commencement of the Revolutionary war he enlisted and served during the seven years and only missed being at General Gates' defeat at Camden by being left behind with smallpox. He came to Alabama in 1819; he died September 21, 1832, in Lowndes county, Ala. These facts are obtained from the *Hearne History,* p. 383.

He left many descendants, among them may be mentioned the late Dr. Joseph T. Hearne, physician and planter of St. Clair, Lowndes county.—Mrs. P. H. Mell in *Transactions* of the Alabama Historical Society, vol. iv, p. 543.

HENDRICKS, HILLARY, aged 80, and a resident of Lawrence county; private N. C. Militia; enrolled on October 29, 1833, under act of Congress of June 7, 1832, payment to date from March 4, 1831; annual allownace, $62.50; sums received to date of publication of list, $125.—*Revolutionary Pension Roll,* in Vol. xiv, Sen Doc. 514, 23rd Cong., 1st sess., 1833-34.

HENRY, JAMES, aged 74, and a resident of Tuscaloosa county; private Virginia Militia; enrolled on April 23, 1833, under act of Congress of June 7, 1832, payment to date from

March 4, 1831; annual allowance, $36.44; sums received to date of publication of list, $109.32.—*Revolutionary Pension Roll*, in Vol. xiv, Sen. Doc. 514, 23rd Cong., 1st sess., 1833-34.

HERVEY, JOHN, aged 74, and a resident of Clarke county; private N. C. Militia; enrolled on October 7, 1833, under act of Congress of June 7, 1832, payment to date from March 4, 1831; annual allowance, $35; sums received to date of publication of list, $105.—*Revolutionary Pension Roll*, in Vol. xiv, Sen. Doc. 514, 23rd Cong., 1st sess., 1833-34.

HICKS, JOHN, a resident of St. Clair county; private, particular service not shown; enrolled on April 15, 1833, under act of Congress of June 7, 1832; annual allowance, $26.66; transferred from Georgia.—*Pension Book*, State Branch Bank, Mobile.

HICKS, WILLIAM, aged 77, and a resident of Greene county; private Virginia Continental Line; enrolled on January 15, 1830, under act of Congress of March 18 ,1818, payment to date from January 4, 1830; annual allowance, $96; sums received to date of publication of list, $16; dropped under act May 1, 1820.—*Revolutionary Pension Roll*, in Vol. xiv, Sen. Doc. 514, 23rd Cong., 1st sess., 1833-34.

HIDECKER, JOHN A., aged 86, and a resident of Autauga county; private S. C. Militia; enrolled on January 17, 1834, under act of Congress of June 7, 1832, payment to date from March 4, 1831; annual allowance, $40.—*Revolutionary Pension Roll*, in Part 3, Vol. xiii, Sen. Doc. 514, 23rd Cong., 1st sess., 1833-34. He resided in Pike county, June 1, 1840, with Sarah Reeks, aged 93.—*Census of Pensioners*, 1841, p. 49.

HIGHTOWER, JOHN. "Mr. John Hightower recently died in Marengo county, Alabama, at the age of 126 years. He received a wound in the battle of Braddock's defeat 99 years ago, and was a soldier in the Revolution. His age can be established by an authentic family record."—*Southern Advocate*, Huntsville, Ala., Nov. 29, 1844.

HILDRETH, REUBEN.—"Died—At his residence in this county, on Saturday 11th inst., Mr. Reuben Hildreth, in the 96th year of his age.

"Mr. Hildreth was a Revolutionary veteran and served his country well in war and peace. He reared a large family, and lived to see his children all happily settled in life."—*Ma-*

Revolutionary Soldiers in Alabama. 55

rengo Ledger, reprinted in *Alabama Beacon,* Greensboro, Ala., Oct. 25, 1845.

HILL, JOEL, aged 72, and a resident of Limestone county; private N. C. Militia; enrolled on February 21, 1833, under act of Congress of June 7, 1832, payment to date from March 4, 1831; annual allowance, $26.66; sums received to date of publication of list, $79.98.—*Revolutionary Pension Roll,* in Vol. xiv., Sen. Doc. 514, 23rd Cong., 1st sess., 1833-34.

HILLHOUSE, WILLIAM, aged 75, and a resident of Marengo county; private, sergeant and lieutenant S. C. Militia; enrolled on March 3, 1834, under act of Congress of June 7, 1832, payment to date from March 4, 1831; annual allowance, $200; sums received to date of publication of list, $600.—*Revolutionary Pension Roll,* in Vol. xiv, Sen. Doc. 514, 23rd Cong., 1st sess., 1833-34. He resided in Greene county, June 1, 1840, aged 81.—*Census of Pensioners,* 1841, p. 149.

HILLSMAN, JOSE. At her residence in this county, on the 4th inst., Mrs. Elizabeth Hillsman, widow of the late Jose Hillsman, formerly of Amelia county, Va., in her 84th year. Her husband was a soldier of the Revolution, and she was the last revolutionary pensioner of the General Government in this county. She was baptized in the Episcopal church in Virginia, about the year 1800, and died professing repentance towards God and faith in the Lord Jesus Christ.—*The Southern Advocate,* Huntsville, Ala., Sept. 24, 1857.

HOFSTALAR, GEORGE, aged 71, and a resident of Blount county; private N. C. Continental Line; enrolled on November 22, 1833, under act of Congress of June 7, 1832, payment to date from March 4, 1831; annual allowance, $77.50; sums received to date of publication of list, $232.50.—*Revolutionary Pensoin Roll,* in Part 3, Vol. xiii, Sen. Doc. 514, 23rd Cong., 1st sess., 1833-34. Spelled also Huffstullar, and was a resident of Blount county, June 1, 1840, aged 76.—*Census of Pensioners,* 1840, p. 148.

HOGAN, CORDELL, a resident of Mobile county; private, particular service not shown; enrolled on March 4, 1831, under act of Congress of June 7, 1832, payment to date from March 4, 1831; annual allowance, $30.—*Pension Book,* State Branch Bank, Mobile.

HOLLADAY, DANIEL, a resident of Marion county; sergeant, particular service not shown; enrolled on December 28, 1835, under act of Congress of June 7, 1832, payment to date from March 4, 1831; annual allowance, $120.—*Pension Book, State Branch Bank, Mobile.*

HOLLAND, CHARLES, aged 76, and a resident of Tuscaloosa county; private S. C. Militia; enrolled on July 2, 1833, under act of Congress of June 7, 1832, payment to date from March 4, 1831; annual allowance, $80; sums received to date of publication of list, $240.—*Revolutionary Pension Roll,* in Vol. xiv, Sen. Doc. 514, 23rd Cong., 1st sess., 1833-34.

HOLLAND, JACOB, came from South Carolina, and is buried at Hebron churchyard, in Greene county. The following inscription is upon his tombstone:

Sacred to the
memory of
JACOB & SARAH HOLLAND
Jacob
departed this life
Oct. 1st, 1852,
Aged 91 years.
Sarah
May 13th, 1851,
Aged 87 years.

—Mrs. P. H. Mell in *Transactions* of the Alabama Historical Society, vol. iv, p. 544.

HOLLAND, JOHN, aged 68, and a resident of Sumter county; private S. C .State Troops; enrolled on April 17, 1834, under act of Congress of June 7, 1832, payment to date from March 4, 1831; annual allowance, $80.—*Revolutionary Pension Roll,* in Vol. xiv, Sen. Doc. 514, 23rd Cong., 1st sess., 1833-34.

HOLLAND, THOMAS, aged 71, and a resident of Limestone county; private S. C. Militia; enrolled on June 13, 1833, under act of Congress of June 7, 1832, payment to date from March 4, 1831; annual allowance, $76.66.; sums received to date of publication of list, $229.98.—*Revolutionary Pension Roll,* in Vol. xiv, Sen. Doc. 514, 23rd Cong., 1st sess., 1833-34. He resided in Limestone county, June 1, 1840, aged 78.—*Census of Pensioners,* 1841, p. 148.

HOLLINGSHEAD, BENJAMIN, aged 72, and a resident of Bibb county; private N. C. State Troops; enrolled on March 5, 1833, under act of Congress of June 7, 1832, payment to date from Marh 4, 1831; annual allowance, $40; sums received to date of publication of list, $100.—*Revolutionary*

Revolutionary Soldiers in Alabama. 57

Pension Roll, Part 3, Vol xiii, Sen. Doc. 514, 23rd Cong., 1st sess., 1833-34.

HOLT, CHARLES, aged 72, and a resident of Blount county; private S. C. Militia; enrolled on October 29, 1833, under act of Congress of June 7, 1832, payment to date from March 4, 1831; annual allowance, $28.33; sums received to date of publication of list, $84.99.—*Revolutionary Pension Roll,* in Part 3, Vol. xiii, Sen. Doc. 514, 23rd Cong., 1st sess., 1833-34. He resided in Blount county, June 1, 1840, aged 78. —*Census of Pensioners,* 1841, p. 148.

HONEY, TOBIAS, aged 78, resided in Calhoun (then Benton) county, June 1, 1840, with Abel Brooks.—*Census of Pensioners,* 1841, p. 148.

HOOKS, CHARLES. "Charles Hooks is buried in Montgomery county, about twenty miles from the city of Montgomery, in a family burial ground on his plantation. It is now known as the 'Old Moulton Place.' His services in the Revolution in North Carolina are mentioned in Wheeler's *History of North Carolina,* and Mrs. Ellet's *Women of the Revolution.* There is an interesting chapter in the latter book, called 'Mary Slocumb,' which gives a delightful account of the beautiful home and patriotic deeds of Mary Hooks Slocumb, elder sister of Charles Hooks. Her husband was Lieutenant Ezekiel Slocumb, who raised a troop of light horse to watch the enemy and punish the Tories. In April, 1781, just after the battle of Guilford Court House, the British colonel, Tarleton, made his headquarters at the Slocumb home in Wayne county. Charles Hooks, a lad of thirteen at the time, was away with his brother-in-law, Lieut. Slocumb, in hot pursuit of some Tory marauders. They narrowly escaped being captured upon their return, as they were ignorant of the fact that a thousand men were in possession of their home, but the warning of a faithful slave enabled them to retreat with safety.

"Charles Hooks was born in Bertie county, North Carolina, February 20th, 1768. and died in Montgomery county, Alabama, on the 18th of October, 1843. After the Revolution he married Mary Ann Hunter; she was the daughter of Isaac Hunter and Priscilla ———, and granddaughter of Isaac Hunter of Chowan, N. C., who died in 1752, and whose will is on file among the records at Edenton, N. C.

Charles Hooks became a man of distinction. He went to the legislature from Duplin county in 1802-03-04 and again in 1810-11. He served seven years as a member of Congress in 1816-17 and again from 1819 to 1825. He moved to Alabama in 1826.

The descent of Charles Hooks is as follows:

(1) William Hooks, of Chowan county, North Carolina, who died in 1751 at an advanced age. Issue: William and John.

(2) John Hooks died in 1732; his wife was Ruth ———; several children, among others,

(3) Thomas Hooks, who married (1) Anna ———, and had children, Mary, Charles and one other; married (2) Mrs. John Charles Slocumb.

Many descendants of Charles Hooks are living in Alabama."
—Mrs. P. H. Mell in the *Transactions* of the Alabama Historical Society, Vol. iv, pp. 545-6.

HOOPER, OBADIAH, a resident of Pickens county; private, particular service not shown; enrolled on April 14, 1836, under act of Congress of June 7, 1832, payment to date from March 4, 1831; annual allowance, $42.—*Pension Book*, State Branch Bank, Mobile.

HUBBARD, THOMAS, aged 79, and a resident of Morgan county; lieutenant, quartermaster and sergeant Virginia State Troops; enrolled on March 23, 1833, under act of Congress of June 7, 1832, payment to date from March 4, 1831; annual allowance, $296.66; sums received to date of publication of list, $889.98.—*Revolutionary Pension Roll*, in Vol. xiv, Sen. Doc. 514, 23rd Cong., 1st sess., 1833-34. He resided in Morgan county, June 1, 1840, aged 87.—*Census of Pensioners*, 1841, p. 148.

HUFF, JAMES, aged 74, and a resident of Perry county; private Virginia Continental Line and Militia; enrolled on October 29, 1833, under act of Congress of June 7, 1832, payment to date from March 4, 1831; annual allowance, $20.—*Revolutionary Pension Roll*, in Vol. xiv, Sen. Doc. 514, 23rd Cong., 1st sess., 1833-34.

HUGHES, JOSEPH, aged 73, and a resident of Greene county; captain S. C. Militia; enrolled on July 2, 1833, under act of Congress of June 7, 1832; payment to date from March 4, 1831; annual allowance, $480; sums received to date of publication of list, $1,440.—*Revolutionary Pension Roll*, in Vol. xiv, Sen. Doc. 514, 23rd Cong., 1st sess., 1833-34.

Mrs. P. H. Mell in the *Transactions* of the Alabama Historical Society, Vol. iv, pp. 546, 548, presents an interesting account of *Captain* Hughes:

"Col. Joseph Hughes came from Union district, South Carolina, to Greene county, Alabama, in 1825. He was buried at Hebron cemetery in that county. The inscription upon his tomb is as follows:

In memory of
COL. JOSEPH HUGHES,
who departed this life
September 4th, 1834.
Aged 85 years.

"He was twice married; the name of his first wife has not been ascertained. She left seven children; their names were William Wright, Josph, Mary, Martha, Sarah and Jane. Col. Joseph Hughes married for a second wife, Annie Brown of South Carolina; they had three children, Stewart, James and Annie. She was an aunt of Governor Albert G. Brown, of Mississippi. Her brother, John Brown, was killed at the battle of Cowpens. All of the children of Col. Hughes came to Alabama except William, who married and settled in South Carolina, and Wright, who was captain of a steamboat on Broad river in South Carolina. Mary married —— Kennedy; Martha, —— Morris; Sarah, —— Maberry; Jane, —— Bruner; Annie, —— White.

"Col. Hughes was a consistent member of the Presbyterian church. He is well remembered by Mrs. Jay, of Benevola, Ala., who is now (1904) in her ninetieth year. She has often heard him speak of his experiences in the Revolutionary war and she has seen and handled his sword and pistol which were sacredly preserved because of their Revolutionary associations.

"Some of the brave exploits of Lieut. Joseph Hughes are described in Saye's *Memoir of McJunkin;* an interesting biographical sketch of him may be found in a pamphlet entitled *The Life of Col. James D. Williams* (1898), by Rev. J. D. Bailey; and several notices of Capt. Joseph Hughes occur in Draper's *King's Mountain and its Heroes,* from which the following brief account of his life is taken, pp. 122, 129, 131-33, 277.

"'He was born in what is now Chester county, South Carolina, in 1761, his parents having retired there temporarily from the present region of Union county, on account of Indian troubles. He served in 1776 on Williamson's Cherokee expedition and subsequently in Georgia. Governor Rutledge, early in 1780, commissioned him as a lieutenant and he fought under Sumter at Rocky Mount and Hanging Rock; and then shared in the heroic action of Musgrove's Mill. His daredevil character and adventurous services in the up-country region of South Carolina during the summer and autumn of 1780 have already been related.

"'Then we find him taking part in the memorable engagements at King's Mountain, Hammond's Store and Cowpens. Though yet a lieutenant, he commanded his company in this latter action. He was not only a man of great personal strength, but of remarkable fleetness on foot. As his men with others broke at the Cowpens and fled before Tarleton's cavalry; and though receiving a sabre cut across his right hand, yet with his drawn sword, he would out-run his men, and passing them, face about and command them to stand, striking right and left to enforce obedience to orders; often repeating with a loud voice: 'You d—d cowards, halt and fight,—there is more danger in running than in fighting, and if you don't stop and fight you will all be killed.

"'But most of them were for a while too demoralized to realize the situation or to obey their officers. As they would scamper off, Hughes would renewedly pursue and once more gaining their front would repeat his tactics to bring them to their duty. At length the company was induced to make a stand on the brow of a slope, some distance from the battle line behind a clump of young pines that partially concealed and protected them from Tarleton's cavalry. Others now joined them for self-protection. Their guns were loaded quickly and they were themselves again. Morgan galloped up and spoke words of encouragement to them. The next moment the British cavalry were at them; but the Whigs reserved their fire till the enemy were so near that it was terribly effective, emptying many a British saddle, when the survivors recoiled. Now Colonel Washington gave them a charge —the battle was restored when Howard with his Marylanders with the bayonet, swept the field. Tarleton acknowledges that 'an unexpected fire from the Americans, who came about as they were retreating, stopped the British and threw them into confusion' when a panic ensued and then a general fight. It was a high and worthy compliment from his old commander, Colonel Brandon, who declared that at the Cowpens 'Hughes saved the fate of the day.'

"'As a deserved recognition of these meritorious services he was promoted to a captaincy early in 1781, when he was scarcely twenty years of age and led his company with characteristic valor at the battle of Eutaw Springs. The Tories had killed his father during the war and many a dear friend, and his animosity against the whole race was alike bitter and unrelenting. In 1825 he removed to Alabama, first to Greene county and then to Pickens, where he died in September, 1834, in his seventy-fourth year. For more than twenty of the closing years of his life he was an elder in the Presbyterian church and the rough and almost tigerlike partisan became as humble and submissive as a lamb. He rose to the rank of colonel in the militia. He was tall and commanding in his appearance, jovial and affable in conversation; yet his early military training rendered him to the last stern and rigid in discipline. In all that makes up the man he was a noble specimen of the Revolutionary hero.'"

HUGHES, WILLIAM, aged 82, and a resident of Shelby county; private N. C. Militia; enrolled on May 24, 1833, under act of Congress of June 7, 1832, payment to date from March 4, 1831; annual allowance, $80.—*Revolutionary Pension Roll,* in Vol. xiv, Sen. Doc. 514, 23rd Cong., 1st sess., 1833-34.

HUSBANDS, WILLIAM, aged 75, and a resident of Greene county; private N. C. Militia; enrolled July 2, 1833, under act of Congress of June 7, 1832, payment to date from March 4, 1831; annual allowance, $80; sums received to date of publication of list, $240.—*Revolutionary Pension Roll,* in Vol. xiv, Sen. Doc. 514, 23rd Cong., 1st sess., 1833-34.

IVEY, ELIJAH, aged 75, and a resident of Lowndes county; private S. C. Militia; enrolled on November 4, 1833, under act of Congress of June 7 ,1832, payment to date from March 4, 1831; annual allowance, $80; sums received to date of publication of list, $200.—*Revolutionary Pension Roll,* in Vol. xiv, Sen. Doc. 514, 23rd Cong., 1st sess., 1833-34.

JACKSON, JOHN, aged 82, and a resident of Jackson county; private S. C. Continental Line; enrolled on November 19, 1819, under act of Congress of March 18, 1818, payment to date from September 21, 1818; annual allowance, $96; sums received to date of publication of list, $1.243.47; transferred from Lincoln county, Tennessee, from March 4, 1816. —*Revolutionary Pension Roll,* in Vol. xiv, Sen. Doc. 514, 23rd Cong., 1st sess., 1833-34.

JAGGERS, JEREMIAH, aged 86, and a resident of Madison county; private S. C. Continental Line; enrolled on February 14, 1824, under act of Congress of March 18, 1818, payment to date from January 28, 1824; annual allowance, $96; sums received to date of publication of list, $730.90.—*Revolutionary Pension Roll,* in Vol. xiv, Sen. Doc. 514, 23rd Cong., 1st sess., 1833-34.

JEEMS, VACHEL, aged 75, and a resident of Lauderdale county; private and sergeant Maryland State Troops; enrolled on May 22, 1824, under act of Congress of June 7, 1832, payment to date from March 4, 1831; annual allowance, $90.27.—*Revolutionary Pension Roll,* in Vol. xiv, Sen. Doc. 514, 23rd Cong., 1st sess., 1833-34.

JENKINS, JOHN, aged 81, and a resident of Limestone county; private and sergeant S. C. Continental Militia; enrolled on June 14, 1833, under act of Congress of June 7, 1832, payment to date from March 4, 1831; annual allowance, $65; sums received to date of publication of list, $195.—*Revolutionary Pension Roll,* in Vol. xiv, Sen. Doc. 514, 23rd Cong., 1st sess., 1833-34.

JENKINS, WILLIAM, aged 73, and a resident of Jackson county; sergeant, lieutenant and captain S. C. State Troops; enrolled on June 6, 1834, under act of Congress of June 7, 1832, payment to date from March 4, 1831; annual allowance, $170.—*Revolutionary Pension Roll,* in Vol. xiv, Sen. Doc. 514, 23rd Cong., 1st sess., 1833-34.

JENNINGS, WILLIAM, a resident of Shelby county; private, particular service not shown; enrolled on August 14, 1833, under act of Congress of June 7, 1832; annual allowance, $26.66; transferred from Tennessee.—*Pension Book,* State Branch Bank, Mobile.

JOHNSON, JOHN, a resident of Pickens county; private, particular service not shown; enrolled on August 1, 1836, under act of Congress of June 7, 1832, payment to date from March 4, 1831; annual allowance, $30.66.—*Pension Book,* State Branch Bank, Mobile.

JOHNSON, RICHARD, aged 74, and a resident of Green county; private Virginia Militia; enrolled on September 18, 1833, under act of Congress of June 7, 1832, payment to date from March 4, 1831; annual allowance, $20.—*Revolutionary Pension Roll,* in Vol. xiv, 23rd Cong., 1st sess., 1833-34. He resided in Greene county, June 1, 1840, aged 79.—*Census of Pensioners,* 1841, p. 149.

JOHNSON, RICHARD, age not given, and a resident of Madison county; Corporal Lee's Legion; enrolled on May 25,

Revolutionary Soldiers in Alabama.   63

1829, under act of Congress of May 15, 1828, payment to date from March 3, 1826; annual allowance, $120; sums received to date of publication of list, $1,020.—*Revolutionary Pension Roll,* in Vol. xiv, Sen. Doc. 514, 23rd Cong., 1st sess., 1833-34. He resided in Madison county, June 1, 1840, aged 82.—*Census of Pensioners,* 1841, p. 148.

JOHNSON, WILLIAM. "On the 23rd inst., at the residence of his son, LEWIS JOHNSON, in this county, WILLIAM JOHNSON, a soldier of the Revolution, in the 87th year of his age. He was a native of Edgefield district, South Carolina, and had resided in this state for a number of years."—*The Dallas Gazette,* Cahaba, April 28, 1854.

JOHNSTON, THOMAS, aged 75, and a resident of St. Clair county; private Virginia Continental Line; enrolled on July 20, 1833, under act of Congress of June 7, 1832, payment to date from March 4, 1831; annual allowance, $40; sums received to date of publication of list, $72.79.—*Revolutionary Pension Roll,* in Vol. xiv, Sen. Doc .514, 23rd Cong., 1st sess., 1833-34.

JONES, FREEMAN, aged 71, and a resident of Pickens county; private Virginia Continental Line; enrolled on August 12, 1833, under act of Congress of June 7, 1832, payment to date from March 4, 1831; annual allowance, $60; sums received to date of publication of list, $180.—*Revolutionary Pension Roll,* in Vol. xiv, Sen. Doc. 514, 23rd Cong., 1st sess., 1833-34.

JONES, JOHN, aged 75, and a resident of Morgan county; private N. C. Continental Line and Militia; enrolled on November 4, 1833, under act of Congress of June 7, 1832, payment to date from March 4, 1831; annual allowance, $61.44; sums received to date of publication of list, $153.60.—*Revolutionary Pension Roll,* in Vol. xiv, Sen. Doc. 514, 23rd Cong., 1st sess., 1833-34.

JONES, JOHN, age not given, a resident of Jackson county; private Alabama Militia; enrolled under acts military establishment, on May 21, 1821, payment to date from April 8, 1820; annual allowance, $48; under act of March 3, 1819, rate reduced to annual allowance of $24.—*Revolutionary Pension Roll,* in Vol. xiv, Sen. Doc. 514, 23rd Cong., 1st sess., 1833-34. (Evidently an erroneous entry.)

JONES, THOMAS C., aged 69, and a resident of Blount county; private S. C. Militia; enrolled on April 8, 1833, under act of Congress of June 7, 1832, payment to date from March 4, 1831; annual allowance, $64.16; sums received to date of publication of list, $192.48.—*Revolutionary Pension Roll,* in Part 3, Vol. xiii, Sen. Doc. 514, 23rd Cong., 1st sess., 1833-34. He resided in Blount county, June 1, 1840, aged 82.—*Census of Pensioners,* 1841, p. 148.

JONES, VINCENT, aged 71, and a resident of Shelby county; private S. C. Militia; enrolled on May 24, 1833, under act of Congress of June 7, 1832; payment to date from March 4, 1831; annual allowance, $23.31; sums received to date of publication of list, $58.28.—*Revolutionary Pension Roll,* in Vol. xiv, Sen. Doc. 514, 23rd Cong., 1st sess., 1833-34.

KEATES, THOMAS, aged 78, and a resident of Tuscaloosa county; private Maryland Continental Line; enrolled on January 10, 1827, under act of Congress of March 18, 1818, payment to date from October 18, 1826; annual allowance, $96; sums received to date of publication of list, $708.64.—*Revolutionary Pension Roll,* in Vol. xiv, Sen. Doc. 514, 23rd Cong., 1st sess., 1833-34.

KELLY, PETER, aged 83, and a resident of Wilcox county; private S. C. Continental Line; enrolled on June 24, 1834, under act of Congress of June 7, 1832, payment to date from March 4, 1831; annual allowance, $50.—*Revolutionary Pension Roll,* in Vol. xiv, Sen. Doc. 514, 23rd Cong., 1st sess., 1833-34.

KENEDA, WILLIAM, aged 78, and a resident of Lauderdale county; private Virginia Militia; enrolled on August 28, 1833, under act of Congress of June 7, 1832, payment to date from March 4, 1831; annual allowance, $34.44; sums received to date of publication of list, $103.32.—*Revolutionary Pension Roll,* in Vol. xiv, Sen. Doc. 514, 23rd Cong., 1st sess., 1833-34.

KENNEDY, DAVID, a resident of Lowndes county; private in cavalry and infantry, particular service not shown; enrolled on February 28, 1837, under act of Congress of June 7, 1832, payment to date from March 4, 1831; annual allowance, $53.10.—*Pension Book,* State Branch Bank, Mobile.

KENNEDY, WILLIAM, age not given, resided in Marion county, June 1, 1840, with J. Kennedy.—*Census of Pensioners,* 1841, p. 148.

KEYES, JOHN WADE.—"The last resting place of this Revolutionary soldier is in an old family burial ground upon

Revolutionary Soldiers in Alabama. 65

his plantation, three miles from Athens on the Huntsville road. His lovely rural home was situated upon a hill about half a mile from Swan creek. His wife, Louisa Talbot Keyes, lies beside him . John Wade Keyes was born in Mystic, near Boston, Mass., Sept. 25, 1752, and died near Athens, Ala., Feb. 13, 1839. His ancestry and many acts of his life are told in a book of the Keyes family called *Solomon Keyes and His Descendants*, by Judge Asa Keyes, of Vermont, published in Battleboro. We find from this that he was the son of Capt. Humphrey Keyes and Marcella Wade. His father was a sea captain of Boston. After many successful voyages he was wrecked and taken captive by the Algerines. He was a prisoner for years, but finally made his escape. Upon his return to Boston he took John, his oldest son, and went down into Virginia. An old family record in Tennessee shows that Capt. Humphrey Keyes in 1775 was proprietor of 'Keyes' Ferry' on the Shenandoah river. A member of the family has now in his possession a letter written by General Washington relative to the survey of Keyes' Ferry tract on the Shenandoah near Charleston, Jefferson county, Virginia. John Wade Keyes married January 27, 1773, in Virginia, Louisa Talbot, niece of President Monroe. She was born near Alexandria, Va., April 20, 1756, and died near Athens, Nov. 6, 1836. This happy couple lived together for sixty-three years.

Early in the Revolutionary war there was a call made for volunteers under Gen. John Thomas in the Shenandoah Valley. John Wade Keyes was the second man to enlist; he was engaged in the battles of Bunker Hill, Lexington, Trenton, White Plains, Princeton, Brandywine and King's Mountain. Capt. John Keyes settled near Alexandria, Virginia, moved thence to the vicinity of Blountsville, Sullivan county, East Tennessee, and finally to Athens, Limestone county, Alabama, where he was one of the pioneer settlers. It is said that he would never consent to apply for a pension and when asked for his reasons he would reply, 'I fought for patriotism, not pensions.' He greatly honored and loved George Washington and he showed his admiration by naming his twin sons for him; one was called George and the other Washington. George Keyes commanded a company under Gen. Jackson and was afterwards made a brigadier-general of militia. Among the descendants of John Wade Keyes were Chancellor Wade Keyes, one of the most prominent jurists that Alabama has produced; George P. Keyes, a noted journalist; Col. John B. Richardson, of New Orleans, commander of the famous

'Washington Artillery' during the war, and others of distinction at the present day."—Mrs. P. H. Mell in *Transactions of the Alabama Historical Society*, Vol. iv, p. 548.

KINARD, JOHN, aged 82, resided in Randolph county, June 1, 1840, with Barnett Kinard.—*Census of Pensioners*, 1841, p. 148.

KINNARD, JOHN, aged 70, and a resident of Marengo county; private S. C. Militia; enrolled on September 5, 1834, under act of Congress of June 7, 1832, payment to date from March 4, 1831; annual allowance, $20.—*Revolutionary Pension Roll*, in Vol. xiv, Sen. Doc. 514, 23rd Cong., 1st sess., 1833-34. He resided in Marengo county, June 1, 1840, aged 77.—*Census of Pensioners*, 1841, p. 149.

KIRBY, ANDREW J., aged 25, resided in Jackson county, June 1, 1840, with John McReynolds.—*Census of Pensioners,* 1841, p. 148.

KIRBY, EPHRAIM. Ephraim Kirby was the first Superior Court judge in what is now Alabama. He was also the first General Grand High Priest of the Royal Arch Masons of the United States, 1798-1804, and he is probably the highest ranking Mason ever buried in Alabama. Judge Kirby was the grandfather of Edmund Kirby Smith, the distinguished Confederate general. The following sketch of his life is condensed from a paper read by Thomas M. Owen before the Alabama State Bar Association, June 29, 1901:

"Mr. Kirby was born Feb. 23, 1757, in Judea Society, Ancient Woodbury, Conn., and was the son of Abraham Kirby, a farmer. The house in which he was born has long since been destroyed, but the land on which it stood is still known as 'the Kirby farm.' About 1763 his parents removed to Litchfield, Conn. His boyhood days were spent in the occupation usually engaging a farmer's lad, but incidents of these years, and of his early education are wanting.

"However, he was trained as a patriot, for on the news of the battle of Lexington, he joined a company of volunteers and arrived at Boston in time to take part in the battle of Bunker Hill. In the latter part of 1776, together with other young men of Litchfield county, he united in forming a company of volunteer cavalry. The men furnished their own horses and equipment; and served about two years. The following is Mr. Kirby's record for this period of service: 'Ephraim Kirby, private, enlisted Dec. 24, 1776, at Litchfield, farmer. Stature 5 ft. 6, complexion dark, eyes dark, hair brown. Discharged Aug. 7, 1778.' His daring and bravery were conspicuous on many fields. He was in many battles and skirmishes. In the engagement at Elk river he received seven sabre cuts on the head, and was left on the field as dead. From the fearful cuts on his head he is said to have lost a portion of his brain, and he was for a long time unconscious. However, his intelligence was suddenly restored, and he at once re-entered the service of his country, continuing active until independence was achieved. At one time he was a lieutenant in a Rhode Island company. In all he is said to have been in nineteen battles and skirmishes, receiving thirteen wounds, including the sabre cuts already mentioned. These honorable evidences of service he carried with him to the grave.

"The Revolutionary War ended, with widened experience and aspiration he set about preparing himself for an enlarged sphere of usefulness. For a while he was a student in Yale College, but he did not graduate. In 1787 his alma mater conferred upon him the degree of master of arts in recognition, doubtless, of his expanding reputation. In Litchfield resided Reynold Marvin, who before the war had been King's attorney, but who had relinquished his official station to throw himself with the cause of the colonists. Determining to embrace the profession of the law, Mr. Kirby entered the office of Mr. Marvin, and under his instruction he was soon admitted to the bar. It was at this time, having entered upon the practice, that he married Ruth Martin, the daughter of his patron and teacher. From this time forth until his removal to the Southwest, although interested in many other matters, he practiced his profession in Litchfield. A fact is now to be noted which is of unusual interest. In 1789 he compiled and published the *Reports of Cases Adjudged in the Superior Court of the State of Connecticut, from the year* 1785, *to May,* 1788, which has the unique distinction of being the first volume of law reports published in America. His work indicates rare legal ability, and is still authority in the courts. Mr. Kirby the same year took the initiative in another matter of great moment. He wrote the pledge and organized the first society, having for its object the promotion of temperance, ever formed in America.

"With a view to bringing about a better condition in the Mississippi Territory, Congress by act of March 27, 1804, provided 'That there shall be appointed an additional judge for the Mississippi Territory, who shall reside at or near the Tombigbee settlement, and who shall possess and exercise, within the district of Washington, * * * the jurisdiction heretofore possessed and exercised by the Superior Court of said Territory,' etc., which jurisdiction was made exclusive, with right of appeal, however, to the Superior Court at Natchez.

"Under this act President Thomas Jefferson, on April 6, 1804, appointed Ephraim Kirby as 'the additional judge.' His commission is as follows, the copy being supplied from the records of the secretary of state at Washington:

THOMAS JEFFERSON,

PRESIDENT OF THE UNITED STATES OF AMERICA.

To all who shall see these Presents, Greeting:

KNOW YE, That reposing special trust and confidence in the Wisdom, Uprightness and Learning of Ephraim Kirby, of Connecticut, and in pursuance of an Act of the Congress of the United States, passed on the twenty-seventh day of March, 1804, entitled 'An Act for the appointment of an additional Judge for the Mississippi Territory, and for other purposes,' I do appoint him the additional Judge for the said Territory to reside at or near the Tombigbee settlement; and do authorize and empower him to execute and fulfill the duties of that Office according to law, and to Have and to Hold the said Office with all the powers, privileges and emoluments to the same of right appertaining during his good behaviour, and to the end of the next Session of the Senate of the United States, and no longer.

In Testimony Whereof, I have caused these letters to be made Patent, and the Seal of the United States to be herunto affixd.

GIVEN under my Hand at the City of Washington, the Sixth day of April, in the year of our Lord one thousand
[SEAL.] eight hundred and four, and of the Independence of the United States of America, the Twenty Eighth.

TH. JEFFERSON.

By the President:
JAMES MADISON,
Secretary of State.

"At best Judge Kirby could not have held more than one term of Court, for he died on Oct. 20, 1804, at Fort Stoddert. As the U. S. government maintained a cantonment there, with a body of soldiers, his remains were interred with all the honors of war and other demonstrations of respect. His body was laid away in the little cemetery to await the last judgment. Mt. Vernon, as is known, is now in the hands of Alabama Insane Hospitals. One of the trustees of this institution, Col. Sam'l Will John, on being told by the writer, some months ago, of his discoveries as to Judge Kirby, made local inquiry at Mt. Vernon in reference to the matter. In response a communication was received by him from Thomas Rogers, of Mt. Vernon, from which the following pertinent extract is made:

"'I arrived in Mt. Vernon Jan. 14, 1850. When I came here I visited Fort Stoddert. I found the remains of chimneys, which were built of sand rock; they have since been removed by negroes. I also found broken delf, and the neck of champagne bottles. In the cemetery, a little north of Fort Stoddert, on the lake, I found a red cedar board, at the head of a grave, with the name nicely cut, 'Ephraim Kirby, died Oct. 4th, [20] 1804.' * * * This board was the only one left to show where the cemetery was. I afterwards visited the place, and found that the board had been destroyed by forest fires.' And so it is that there is now no monument to mark the grave; and indeed the exact location of the grave will be hard to identify.

"In conclusion I think it may with all propriety be claimed that Alabama has a part in the splendid heritage left by this distinguished man. Certainly there is in his life much to emulate. Strong of mind and will, patriotic in all crises, far-seeing and constructive in his mental operations, he towers above scores of his public contemporaries, as does the mountain peak above the hill. He was essentially a pioneer—the first to edit a published volume of official decisions and reports, the founder of the first organized temperance movement in America, and the first Superior Court judge in what is now Alabama. An old lawyer of Litchfield pays this warm tribute to his worth: 'Colonel Kirby was a man of the highest moral as well as physical courage, devoted in his feelings and aspirations, warm, generous, and constant in his attachments, and of indomitable energy. He was withal gentle and winning in his manners, kindly in his disposition, and naturally of an ardent and cheerful temperament, though the last few years of his life were saddened by heavy pecuniary misfortunes. As a lawyer he was remarkable for frankness and downright honesty to his clients, striving to prevent litigation and effecting compromises. He enjoyed the friendship of many of the sages of the Revolution.'"—*Transactions* of the Alabama Historical Society, Vol. iv, pp. 550-553.

KIRKLAND, WILLIAM, aged 72, and a resident of Autauga county; private S. C. State Troops and Militia; enrolled on January 11, 1833, under act of Congress of June 7, 1832, payment to date from March 4, 1831; annual allowance, $72.33; sums received to date of publication of list, $217.—*Revolutionary Pension Roll,* in Part 3, Vol. xiii, Sen. Doc. 514, 23rd Cong., 1st sess., 1833-34.

LACKEY, WILLIAM, aged 80, and a resident of Lawrence county; private Virginia Militia; enrolled on April 23, 1833, under act of Congress of June 7, 1832, payment to date from March 4, 1831; annual allowance, $79.78; sums received to date of publication of list, $239.34.—*Revolutionary Pension Roll,* in Vol. xiv, Sen. Doc. 514, 23rd Cong., 1st sess., 1833-34. He resided in Lawrence county, June 1, 1840, aged 87.—*Census of Pensioners,* 1841, p. 148.

LAFOY, JAMES, a resident of Washington county; private in infantry and cavalry, particular service not shown; enrolled on September 9, 1836, under act of Congress of June 7, 1832, payment to date from March 4, 1831; annual allowance, $25.—*Pension Book,* State Branch Bank, Mobile.

LANDERS, JOHN, aged 82, resided in Benton county, June , 1840.—*Census of Pensioners,* 1841, p. 148.

LANGLEY, JAMES, aged 80, resided in Chambers county, June 1, 1840.—*Census of Pensioners,* 1841, p. 149.

LANSDALE, ISAAC, a resident of Montgomery county; private Delaware Line; enrolled on September 9, 1828, under act of Congress of May 15, 1828, payment to date from March 3, 1826; annual allowance, $80; sums received to date of publication of list, $720.—*Revolutionary Pension Roll,* in Vol. xiv, Sen. Doc. 514, 23rd Cong., 1st sess., 1833-34. He resided in Fayette county, June 1, 1840, aged 80.—*Census of Pensioners,* 1841, p. 148.

LATTY, JOHN. "On the 30th ult., JAMES LATTY, an old citizen of this county in the 102nd year of his age. He was a native of North Carolina, but had lived on the head waters of Brierfork for two generations. He volunteered in the revolutionary war; but his father, being in a helpless condition, furnished means for a substitute for his son."—*The Southern Advocate,* Huntsville, April 11, 1860.

LAVENDER, HUGH, aged 79, and a resident of Greene county; dragoon S. C. Militia; enrolled on February 10, 1834, under act of Congress of June 7, 1832, payment to date from March 4, 1831; annual allowance, $66.21.—*Revolutionary Pension Roll,* in Vol. xiv, Sen. Doc. 514, 23rd Cong., 1st sess., 1833-34.

LENTZ, HENRY, aged 81, and a resident of Limestone county; private and sergeant N. C. Militia; enrolled on June 14, 1833, under act of Congress of June 7, 1832, payment to date from March 4, 1831; annual allowance, $59.33; sums received to date of publication of list, $148.32.—*Revolutionary Pension Roll,* in Vol. xiv, Sen. Doc. 514, 23rd Cong., 1st sess., 1833-34.

LEWIS, AARON, aged 75, and a resident of Clarke county; private S. C. Continental Line; enrolled on April 20, 1833, under act of Congress of June 7, 1832, payment to date from March 4, 1831; annual allowance, $53.33; sums received to date of publication of list, $160.—*Revolutionary Pension Roll,* Vol. xiv, Sen. Doc. 514, 23rd Cong., 1st sess., 1833-34. He resided in Pike county, June 1, 1840, aged 80.—*Census of Pensioners,* 1841, p. 149.

LEWIS, AXIOM, aged 75, resided in Clarke county, June 1, 1840, with William R. Hamilton.—*Census of Pensioners,* 1841, p. 149.

LINDSAY, DAVID. A revolutionary soldier of this name is buried at Elliottsville, Shelby county, but no facts as to his age or service have been ascertained.

LINDSAY, JAMES, a resident of Marion county; private, particular service not shown; enrolled on August 22, 1835, under act of Congress of June 7, 1832, payment to date from March 4, 1831; annual allowance, $20.—*Pension Book,* State Branch Bank, Mobile.

LINTON, JOHN, aged 76 years, and a resident of Butler county; private N. C. Militia and State Troops; enrolled on Oct. 19, 1833, under act of Congress of June 7, 1832, payment to date from March 4, 1831; annual allowance, $76.66.—*Revolutionary Pension Roll,* in Part 3, Vol. xiii, Sen. Doc. 514, 23rd Cong., 1st sess., 1833-34. He resided in Butler county, June 1, 1840, with Hugh Linton, aged 82.—*Census of Pensioners,* 1841, p. 149.

LITTLETON, CHARLES, aged 74, and a resident of Lauderdale county; private Georgia Militia; enrolled on October 29, 1833, under act of Congress of June 7, 1832, payment to date from March 4, 1831; annual allowance, $80.—*Revolutionary Pension Roll*, in Vol. xiv, Sen. Doc. 514, 23rd Cong., 1st sess., 1833-34. He resided in Lauderdale county, June 1, 1840, aged 79.—*Census of Pensioners*, 1841, p. 148.

Of him Mrs. P. H. Mell in *Transactions* of the Alabama Historical Society, Vol. iv, p. 554, says:

"This soldier was from Maryland or Virginia. He rests in a little country graveyard, fifteen miles from Florence, in Lauderdale county, Alabama. This graveyard is nearly a mile from Bethel Grove Methodist church; the church being on Middle Cypress creek. He drew a pension and his grave is marked by a stone which bears this inscription:

CHARLES LITTLETON.
Revolutionary Soldier.
Died March 29th, 1848, at 3 o'clock P. M.
Aged about 103 or 105 years.

"A descendant gives information that Charles Littleton was the son of Solomon Littleton, an Englishman, who owned land at or near Washington City, and is said to have built the first house on the site of Washington. He joined the rebellious colonists and, in revenge, the English captured him and placed him in a smallpox hospital at Ninety-Six, South Carolina, and thus took his life."

LIVING, STEPHEN, sen., aged 80, resided in Pike county, June 1, 1840.—*Census of Pensioners*, 1841, p. 149.

LIVINGSTON, SAMUEL, aged 76, and a resident of Morgan county; private N. C. Militia; enrolled on July 2, 1833, under act of Congress of June 7, 1832, payment to date from March 4, 1831; annual allowance, $21.67; sums received to date of publication of list, $61.01.—*Revolutionary Pension Roll*, in Vol. xiv, Sen. Doc. 514, 23rd Cong., 1st sess., 1833-34.

LOFTON, THOMAS, aged 73, and a resident of Pickens county; private, captain and sergeant S. C. Militia; enrolled on February 2, 1833, under act of Congress of June 7, 1832, payment to date from March 4, 1831; annual allowance, $340; sums received to date of publication of list, $1,020 —*Revolutionary Pension Roll*, in Vol. xiv, Sen. Doc. 514, 23rd Cong., 1st sess., 1833-34.

He came from Pendleton district, South Carolina, to Alabama. The young people of his neighborhood knew him as "Grandsire Lofton" and loved him for his kind and genial disposition; some are still living who remember his interesting stories of the Revolution. He was a member of the Presbyterian church. He is buried at Bethesda church near Benevola; no stone marks his last resting place.—Mrs. P. H. Mell in *Transactions* of the Alabama Historical Society, Vol. iv, p. 554.

LONG, DANIEL, aged 80, and a resident of Madison county; dragoon Virginia Continental Line; enrolled on November 22, 1833, under act of Congress of June 7, 1832, payment to date from March 4, 1831; annual allowance, $100; sums received to date of publication of list, $300.—*Revolutionary Pension Roll,* in Vol. xiv, Sen. Doc. 514, 23rd Cong., 1st sess., 1833-34.

LOOKINGBILL, DANIEL, age not given, a resident of Dallas county; private 14th U. S. Regular; enrolled on July 30, 1831, payment to date from July 25, 1831; annual allowance, $96; sums received to date of publication of list, $250.89; Acts Military establishment.—*Revolutionary Pension Roll,* in Vol. xiv, Sen. Doc. 514, 23rd Cong., 1st sess., 1833-34. Resided also in Marion, Fayette and Tuscaloosa counties.—*Pension Book,* State Branch Bank, Mobile.

LUCAS, JAMES. Mary, wife of James Lucas, a resident of Montgomery county; enrolled on January 12, 1838, under act of Congress of June 7, 1832, payment to date from March 4, 1831; annual allowance, $600.—*Pension Book,* State Branch Bank, Mobile. She rsided in Montgomery county, June 1, 1840, with Jane W. Freeney, aged 80.—*Census of Pensioners,* 1841, p. 149.

LUCAS, JOHN, private, particular service not shown; enrolled on January 10, 1837, under act of Congress of June 7, 1832; annual allowance, $20; no record of any payment being made.—*Pension Book,* State Branch Bank, Mobile.

LUCAS, RANDOLPH, private, particular service not shown; enrolled on January 10, 1837, under act of Congress of June 7, 1832; annual allowance, $20; no record of any payment having been made.—*Pension Book,* State Branch Bank, Mobile.

LYLE, JOHN, aged 84, resided in Covington county, June 1, 1840, with John B. Dixon.—*Census of Pensioners,* 1841, p. 149.

LYNN, JAMES, aged 70, and a resident of Morgan county; private N. C. Continental Line; enrolled on September 24, 1833, under act of Congress of June 7, 1832, payment to date from March 4, 1831; annual allowance, $74.33; sums received to date of publication of list, $222.99.—*Revolutionary Pension Roll,* in Vol. xiv, Sen. Doc. 514, 23rd Cong., 1st sess., 1833-34. He resided in Morgan county, June 1, 1840, aged 76.—*Census of Pensioners,* 1841, p. 148.

MABERRY, GEORGE, aged 82, resided in Bibb county, June 1, 1840.—*Census of Pensioners,* 1841, p. 149.

MABGLY, VARDER, aged 102, resided in Walker county, June 1, 1840, with Robert Mabgly.—*Census of Pensioners,* 1841, p. 150.

McCALL, JOHN, aged 70, and a resident of Limestone county; private and sergeant N. C. Continental Line; enrolled on Jnauary 5, 1833, under act of Congress of June 7, 1832, payment to date from March 4, 1831; annual allowance, $20; sums received to date of publication of list, $60.—*Revoutionary Pension Roll,* in Vol. xiv, Sen. Doc. 514, 23rd Con., 1st sess., 1833-34.

McCARTER, JAMES, aged 69, and a resident of Greene county; private S. C. Militia; enrolled on Nov. 4, 1833, under act of Congress of June 7, 1832, payment to date from March 4, 1831; annual allowance, $80; sums received to date of publication of list, $200.—*Revolutionary Pension Roll,* in Vol. xiv, Sen. Doc. 514, 23rd Cong., 1st sess., 1833-34. He resided in Greene county, June 1, 1840, aged 76.—*Census of Pensioners,* 1841, p. 149.

McCARTNEY, JOHN, aged 75, and a resident of Madison county; private N. C. Militia; enrolled on July 2, 1833, under act of Congress of June 7, 1832, payment to date from March 4, 1831; annual allowance, $51.34; sums received to date of publication of list, $128.35.—*Revolutionary Pension Roll,* in Vol. xiv, Sen. Doc. 514, 23rd Cong., 1st sess., 1833-34.

McCARTY, MICHAEL, aged 90, resided in Jefferson county, June 1, 1840.—*Census of Pensioners,* 1841, p. 149.

McCARY, RICHARD, aged 81, and a resident of Bibb county; private Virginia Continental Line; enrolled on June 12, 1819, under act of Congress of March 18, 1818, payment to date from May 3, 1819; annual allowance, $96; sums received to date of publication of list, $1,497.31; transferred from Edegfield district, S. C., from March 4, 1827.—*Revolutionary Pension Roll,* in Vol. xiv, Sen. Doc. 514, 23rd Cong.,

Revolutionary Soldiers in Alabama. 75

1st sess., 1833-34. Also resided in Washington county.—*Pension Book,* State Branch Bank, Mobile.

McCLURE, JOHN, aged 76, and a resident of Limestone county; private and sergeant N. C. Militia; enrolled on May 10, 1834, under act of Congress of June 7, 1832, payment to date from March 4, 1831; annual allowance, $80.—*Revolutionary Pension Roll,* in Vol. xiv, Sen. Doc. 514, 23rd Cong., 1st sess., 1833-34.

McCONNELL, JAMES, sen., aged 83, resided in Limestone county, June 1, 1840.—*Census of Pensioners,* 1841, p. 148.

McCORMACK, BENJAMIN, aged 89, and a resident of Perry county; private Georgia Militia; enrolled on September 17, 1833, under act of Congress of June 7, 1832, payment to date from March 4, 1831; annual allowance, $90; sums received to date of publication of list, $270.—*Revolutionary Pension Roll,* in Vol. xiv, Sen. Doc. 514, 23rd Cong., 1st sess., 1833-34.

McCORMACK, JOS. R., aged 96, resided in Jackson county, June 1, 1840.—*Census of Pensioners,* 1841, p. 148.

McCOSKLIN, ——, aged 78, resided in Sumter county, June 1, 1840.—*Census of Pensioners,* 1841, p. 149.

McCRAVY, JOHN, aged 87, resided in Jackson county, June 1, 1840, with Thomas Coleman.—*Census of Pensioners,* 1841, p. 148.

McCRORY, JAMES. "James McCrory is buried in a cemetery at 'Old Bethany Church' (Primitive Baptist), near the town of Vienna in Pickens county. The following inscription is on his tombstone :

In Memory of
JAMES M'CRORY.
Died Nov. 24th, 1840, aged 82 years,
6 mo. and 9 days.
Deceased was a soldier of the Revolution and was at the battles of Germantown, Brandywine and Guilford Courthouse, and was one of Washington's lifeguard at Valley Forge and served his country faithfully during the war.
Peace to the soldiers' dust.

"The following account of him is copied from the *Tuscaloosa Flag of the Union,* December, 1840:

"'James McCrory was born May 15, 1758, at Larga, on the river Bann, in the county of Antrim, Ireland. He sailed from Belfast in 1775 when he was 17 years old and landed at Baltimore July 1st, in the same year. In 1776 he settled in Guilford county, N. C., and enlisted in the Continental army in the same year. He was at the battle of Brandywine, September 11, 1777, under General Washington at the battle of Germantown, and wintered at Valley Forge in 1777-78. Subsequently he fought under General Greene at Guilford Court House, March 15, 1781, was in the battle of Eutaw Springs, and in the battle of Stono. He was with General Gates at his defeat at Camden and with General Morgan in the glorious victory at the Cowpens. For courage, good service and meritorious conduct he was promoted to the rank of ensign in the Life Guard of General Washington, and while acting in this capacity, he was taken prisoner and confined on board a prison ship for six months. He came to Alabama while it was yet a territory, and made his home at Tuscaloosa for the last twenty-five years of his life. This true patriot died November 24, 1840, at the age of eighty-two.'

"There is a list of North Carolina Continental troops published in the *N. C. Historical and Genealogical Register,* on p. 424 of which we find the name of James McCrory, ensign in the Ninth regiment, under Col. John P. Williams, May 2, 1777. Thomas McCrory was a captain in the same regiment. The services of James McCrory are also stated in the proceedings of the 27th Congress, 2d Session, in the Senate, February 4th, 1842, report of the Committee on Revolutionary Claims:

"'James McCrory was a sergeant in Capt. Cook's company of the 9th regiment, enlisted on the 15th day of April, 1776, for the term of three years; on the 2d day of May, 1777, he was promoted to the rank of ensign. In January 1778, the nine regiments which composed the line, being reduced to three, the supernumerary officers were sent home, of which he was one. He then joined the nine months' men and marched to the south and was at the battle of Stono, the 30th of June, 1779, and was at Gates' defeat in August, 1780, and was taken prisoner on the 24th of February, 1781, by Tarleton's dragoons and was kept prisoner four months at Wilmington and then paroled; and in November, 1782, he took prisoner Colonel Bryant, a British officer, and gave him up to a regular officer of the American army.'

"In spite of this array of gallant services the committee reported adversely because of some technicality; but as the old hero had then been dead two years he was probably not very deeply affected or disappointed by the decision."—Mrs. P. H. Mell in *Transactions* of the Alabama Historical Society, Vol. iv, pp. 554-556.

Revolutionary Soldiers in Alabama. 77

Details of his service: He was an ensign 9th Regular N. C. Line; enrolled on June 13, 1829, under act of Congress of May 15, 1828, payment to date from March 3, 1826; annual allowance, $240; sums received to date of publication of list, $2,160; John McCrory, agent.—*Revolutionary Pension Roll,* in Vol. xiv, Sen. Doc. 514, 23rd Cong., 1st sess., 1833-34. He resided in Pickens county, June 1, 1840, with Robert McCrory, aged 82.—*Census of Pensioners,* 1841, p. 149.

McCUTCHEN, JOHN, aged 78, and a resident of Jackson county; private N. C. Militia; enrolled on January 2, 1834, under act of Congress of June 7, 1832, payment to date from March 4, 1831; annual allowance, $80.—*Revolutionary Pension Roll,* in Vol. xiv, Sen. Doc. 514, 23rd Cong., 1st sess., 1833-34. The following interesting account is extracted from the *Southern Advocate,* Huntsville, Jan. 27, 1835.

"JACKSON COUNTY, ALA., JAN. 19, 1835.

"It is our unhappy lot to anonunce that another *Revolutionary Hero* has gone! COL. JOHN MCCUTCHEN, who, in 'the times that tried men's souls,' stood boldly forth in defense of the liberty and independence of his country, bidding defiance not only to oppression, but confronting the armed myrmidons of the Tyrant, was on the 17th (inst.) in the eightieth year of his age, summoned to 'another and a better world.'

"He engaged early in the Revolutionary conflict, was at the defense of Fort Moultrie, the battle at Eutaw Springs, and with a true patriotic zeal participated in all the perils and distress that so peculiarly characterized the unfeeling warfare, then waged throughout the Carolinas; nor did he retire until he had the satisfaction of beholding the independence of his country, for which he had so long and ardently struggled, permanently secured.

"Having devoted his youth to the service of his country in the field, in the maturity of manhood he engaged with those fearless and enterprising pioneers, who emigrating to the West, embarked in the arduous undertaking of reclaiming the fertile valley of the Tennessee from its then savage wilderness, and preparing it for the enjoyment of all the arts, luxuries and refinements of social life.

"He has ever been noted as a man of uncommon intellectual endowments—for the last forty years has been a professor of christianity of the Baptist order, and been esteemed by all as a worthy example and an honor to his profession. Thus ripe in years and rich in the consciousness of having at two different periods of his life, rendered important services to his country, and in the consoling hopes of a glorious immortality, the *veteran* has departed, leaving his relatives and numerous friends to mourn his loss.

"On Monday the 19th inst., as the citizens of this vicinity had convened to pay the last honors to the deceased, on motion of Maj. *John B. Stevens*, they constituted themselves into a meeting, for the purpose of making a public manifestation of their grief, to acknowledge the services, and express the high regard they have ever entertained for the principles of their departed friend. Col. *James Smith* was called to the chair and Maj. *John B. Stevens* appointed secretary—when the following resolutions were unanimously adopted, viz:

"*Resolved,* That, under a deep sense of the gratitude we owe to those sages and heroes who achieved our independence, we deem it a duty incumbent upon us, their sons, with a filial piety to pay every tribute of respect to their virtues and their valor, as the only remuneration in our power, for the manifold rights and privileges that we now enjoy.

"*Resolved,* That in the death of Col. *John McCutchen,* we have to lament the loss of one of that band of *aged warriors,* whose presence never fails to enliven our zeal in the cause of liberty and to remind us what it cost—that in him we have lost a firm patriot, a worthy citizen, a pious christian and an esteemed friend. And while we respectfully acknowledge his public services, stern integrity and private worth, we deeply sympathize with his *widow* and other members of his family in their bereavement.

"*Resolved,* That the above resolutions be signed by the Chairman and Secretary, and transmitted to the Democrat and Southern Advocate for publication.

"JAMES SMITH, *Chairman.*"
"JOHN B. STEVENS, *Secretary.*"

McDERMENT, JOS., aged 83, resided in Blount county, June 1, 1840, with John Cook.—*Census of Pensioners,* 1841, p. 148.

McDEARMON, THOMAS, aged 82, and a resident of Jackson county; private S. C. Militia; enrolled on January 17, 1834, under act of Congress of June 7, 1832, payment to date from March 4, 1831; annual allowance, $34.44; sums received to date of publication of list, $103.32.—*Revolutionary Pension Roll,* in Vol. xiv, Sen. Doc. 514, 23rd Cong., 1st sess., 1833-34.

McDONALD, JOHN, aged 81, resided in Jefferson county, June 1, 1840, with Launcelot Armstrong.—*Census of Pensioners,* 1841, p .149.

(354)

Revolutionary Soldiers in Alabama. 79

McDONELL, JAMES, aged 82, resided in Lawrence county, June 1 ,1840.—*Census of Pensioners,* 1841, p. 148. Resided also in Pickens county.—*Pension Book,* State Branch Bank, Mobile.

McDOWELL, JOHN, aged 76, and a resident of Morgan county; private Maryland Continental Line; enrolled on April 18, 1833, under act of Congress of June 7, 1832, payment to date from March 4, 1831; annual allowance, $36.66; sums received to date of publication of list, $73.32.—*Revolutionary Pension Roll,* in Vol. xiv, Sen. Doc. 514, 23rd Cong., 1st sess., 1833-34.

McDUFF, DANIEL, a resident of Madison county; captain Regular S. C. Line; enrolled on June 1, 1830, under act of Congress of May 15, 1828, payment to date from March 3, 1836; annual allowance, $480; sums received to date of publication of list, $2,432; W. F. McDuff, administrator; admitted under act of April 2, 1830. Died March 26, 1831.—*Revolutionary Pension Roll,* in Vol. xiv, Sen. Doc. 514, 23rd Cong., 1st sess., 1833-34.

McGAUPHY, SAMUEL, aged 71, and a resident of Lawrence county; private, captain and lieutenant N. C. Militia; enrolled on January 4, 1834, under act of Congress of June 7, 1832, payment to date from March 4, 1831; annual allowance, $233.32; sums received to date of publication of list, $683.30. —*Revolutionary Pension Roll,* in Vol. xiv, Sen. Doc. 514, 23rd Cong., 1st sess., 1833-34. He resided in Lawrence county, June 1, 1840, aged 78.—*Census of Pensioners,* 1841, p. 148.

McGEHEE, WILLIAM, aged 79, and a resident of Jackson county; private Virginia State Troops; enrolled on January 4, 1834, under act of Congress of June 7, 1832, payment to date from March 4, 1831; annual allowance, $30; sums received to date of publication of list, $75.—*Revolutionary Pension Roll,* in Vol. xiv, Sen. Doc. 514, 23rd Cong., 1st sess., 1833-34.

McGUIRE, ELIJAH, aged 77, and a resident of Tuscaloosa county; sergeant S. C. Continental Line; enrolled on December 12, 1827, under act of Congress of March 18, 1818, payment to date from October 12, 1827; annual allowance, $96; sums received to date of publication of list, $56.19.— *Revolutionary Pension Roll,* in Vol. xiv, Sen. Doc. 514, 23rd Cong., 1st sess., 1833-34.

McILKENY, JAMES, age not given, a resident of Madison county; private Virginia Continental Line; enrolled on

May 23, 1820, under act of Congress of March 18, 1818, payment to date from October 8, 1818; annual allowance, $96; suspended under act of May 1, 1820.—*Revolutionary Pension Roll,* in Vol. xiv, Sen. Doc. 514, 23rd Cong., 1st sess., 1833-34.

McINALLY, JONAH, aged 52, resided in Jackson county, June 1, 1840.—*Census of Pensioners,* 1841, p. 148.

McKINNEY, CHARLES, aged 71, and a resident of Limestone county; private and sergeant Virginia Militia; enrolled on June 14, 1833, under act of Congress of June 7, 1832, payment to date from March 4, 1831; annual allowance, $27.33; sums received to date of publication of list, $68.32.—*Revolutionary Pension Roll,* in Vol. xiv, Sen. Doc. 514, 23rd Cong., 1st sess., 1833-34.

McNEELY, DAVID, aged 76, and a resident of Madison county; private Virginia Continental Line and Militia; enrolled on June 13, 1833, under act of Congress of June 7, 1832, payment to date from March 4, 1831; annual allowance, $30.77; sums received to date of publication of list, $92.31.—*Revolutionary Pension Roll,* in Vol. xiv, Sen. Doc. 514, 23rd Cong., 1st sess., 1833-34.

McWHORTER, JOHN, aged 70, and a resident of Lawrence county; private S. C. Militia; enrolled on December 20, 1833, under act of Congress of June 7, 1832; payment to date from March 4, 1831; annual allowance, $80; sums received to date of publication of list, $200.—*Revolutionary Pension Roll,* in Vol. xiv, Sen. Doc. 514, 23rd Cong., 1st sess., 1833-34.

MADISON, JOHN, age not given, a resident of Greene county; corporal 39th Regular U. S. Infantry; enrolled on September 16, 1816; payment to date from July 9, 1814; annual allowance, $96; sums received to $927.16; transferred from Lincoln county, Tennessee, from March 4, 1825; under act of March 3, 1819, to date from March 4, 1824, rate reduced to annual allowance of $64, under which the sum of $640 received to date of publication of list.—*Revolutionary Pension Roll,* in Vol. xiv, Sen. Doc. 514, 23rd Cong., 1st sess., 1833-34.

MADISON, PEYTON, age not given, a resident of Greene county; private 39th Regular U. S. Infantry; enrolled on September 16, 1816; payment to date from July 9, 1814; annual allowance, $48; sums received, $1,023.15; transferred from Bedford county, West Tennessee, from March 4, 1825; under act of March 3, 1819, to date from March 4, 1825, rate reduced to annual allowance of $24, under which the sum of $34.60 received, and April 12, 1826, old rate of $48 annual allowance restored, under which the sum of $363.18 received to date of publication of list.—*Revolutionary Pension Roll,* in Vol. xiv, Sen. Doc. 514, 23rd Cong., 1st sess., 1833-34.

MAHARG, ARCHIBALD, aged 71, and a resident of St. Clair county; private S. C. Militia; enrolled on July 24, 1833, under act of Congress of June 7, 1832, payment to date from March 4, 1831; annual allowance, $35; sums received to date of publication of list, $105.—*Revolutionary Pension Roll,* in Vol. xiv, Sen. Doc. 514, 23rd Cong., 1st sess., 1833-34.

MAINYARD, COLEY, aged 74, and a resident of Limestone county; private Virginia Continental Line; enrolled on January 26, 1830, under the act of Congress of March 18, 1818, payment to date from January 2, 1830; annual allowance, $96; sums received to date of publication of list, $352.51.—*Revolutionary Pension Roll,* in Vol. xiv, Sen. Doc. 514, 23rd Cong., 1st sess., 1833-34.

MAJORS, BENJAMIN, a resident of Dallas county; private, particular service not shown; enrolled on August 28, 1834, under act of Congress of June 7, 1832, payment to date from March 4, 1831; annual allowance, $30.—*Pension Book,* State Branch Bank, Mobile.

MALLERY, JOHN, aged 75, and a resident of Limestone county; private and sergeant Virginia State Troops; enrolled on February 23, 1833, under act of Congress of June 7, 1832, payment to date from March 4, 1831; annual allowance, $80; sums received to date of publication of list, $240.—*Revolutionary Pension Roll,* in Vol. xiv, Sen. Doc. 514, 23rd Cong., 1st sess., 1833-34.

MALLORY, JOHN, aged 75, resided in Benton county, June 1, 1840, with Henry H. Mallory.—*Census of Pensioners,* 1841, p. 148.

MALONE, CORNELIUS, aged 76, and a resident of Morgan county; private S. C. Militia; enrolled on July 2, 1833, under act of Congress of June 7, 1832, payment to date from March 4, 1831; annual allowance, $63.33; sums received to date of publication of list, $189.99.—*Revolutionary Pension Roll,* in Vol. xiv, Sen. Doc. 514, 23rd Cong., 1st sess., 1833-34. He resided in Morgan county, June 1, 1840, aged 81.—*Census of Pensioners,* 1841, p. 148.

MALONE, WILLIAM, aged 77, and a resident of Limestone county; private and sergeant S. C. Militia; enrolled on

August 12, 1833, under act of Congress of June 7, 1832, payment to date from March 4, 1831; annual allowance, $90; sums received to date of publication of list, $225.—*Revolutionary Pension Roll*, in Vol. xiv, Sen. Doc. 514, 23rd Cong., 1st sess., 1833-34. He resided in Limestone county, June 1, 1840, aged 85.—*Census of Pensioners*, 1841, p. 148.

MANGUM, JOHN, aged 71, and a resident of Pickens county; private S. C. Militia; enrolled on March 15, 1833, under act of Congress of June 7, 1832, payment to date from March 4, 1831; annual allowance, $60; sums received to date of publication of list, $180.—*Revolutionary Pension Roll*, in Vol. xiv, Sen. Doc. 514, 23rd Cong., 1st sess., 1833-34.

MAPLES, WILLIAM C. "DIED—At the residence of his sons, in Madison county, Ala., on the 26th ult., WILLIAM C. MAPLES, in the 81st year of his age. He was a native of Virginia and was one of the Guard, at the age of fifteen years, on Dan River, when the battle was fought at Guilford Court House. He emigrated to East Tennessee in the year 1796, and served as a volunteer in the war of 1812; and emigrated to Alabama in the year 1833. He had been a member of the Baptist church for the rise of fifty years; he was a faithful and useful member of that society, and filled the office of a Deacon and Clerk for the church for a number of years; he was esteemed as a father in the Gospel; a tender husband and an affectionate father to his children; an agreeable and obliging neighbor. He departed this life in the triumph of a living faith—'In the hope of that eternal life which God, that cannot lie, promised before the world began.' He has left a numerous train of connections, scattered almost from the Atlantic to the Pacific ocean.

"The Athens, Tenn., and Lynchburg, Va., papers are requested to copy."—*The Democrat*, (Huntsville), November 17, 1847.

MARKHAM, LEWIS, aged 75, resided in Lauderdale county, June 1, 1840.—*Census of Pensioners*, 1841, p. 148.

MAROM,* HUGH, aged 70, and a resident of Jefferson
*Evidently, "Morrow."
county; private S. C. Militia; enrolled on March 15, 1833, under act of Congress of June 7, 1832, payment to date from March 4, 1831; annual allowance, $20; sums received to date of publication of list, $60.—*Revolutionary Pension Roll*, in Vol. xiv, Sen. Doc. 514, 23rd Cong., 1st sess., 1833-34.

Revolutionary Soldiers in Alabama. 83

MARTIN, ANDREW, aged 86, and a resident of Madison county; private N. C. Continental Line; enrolled on September 26, 1833, under act of Congress of June 7, 1832, payment to date from March 4, 1831; annual allowance, $36.66; sums received to date of publication of list, $91.65.—*Revolutionary Pension Roll*, in Vol. xiv, Sen. Doc. 514, 23rd Cong., 1st sess., 1833-34. He resided in Madison county, June 1, 1840, aged 105.—*Census of Pensioners*, 1841, p. 148.

MARTIN, JAMES, aged 75, and a resident of Greene county, private S. C. Militia; enrolled on September 17, 1833, under act of Congress of June 7, 1832, payment to date from March 4, 1831; annual allowance, $40; sums received to date of publication of list, $120.—*Revolutionary Pension Roll*, in Vol. xiv, Sen. Doc. 514, 23rd Cong., 1st sess., 1833-34.

MARTIN, WILLIAM, a resident of Montgomery county; private, particular service not shown; enrolled on August 21, 1834, payment to date from March 4, 1831; annual allowance, $20.—*Pension Book*, State Branch Bank, Mobile.

MASON, JOHN, aged 72, resided in Mobile county, June 1, 1840.—*Census of Pensioners*, 1841, p. 149.

MATHEWS, BENJAMIN, aged 70, and a resident of Jackson county; private Virginia Continental Line and Militia; enrolled on January 2, 1834, under act of Congress of June 7, 1832, payment to date from March 4, 1831; annual allowance, $46.66; sums received to date of publication of list, $139.98.—*Revolutionary Pension Roll*, in Vol. xiv, Sen. Doc. 514, 23rd Cong., 1st sess., 1833-34. He resided in Jackson county, June 1, 1840, aged 78.—*Census of Pensioners*, 1841, p. 148.

MAYBERRY, GEORGE, aged 74, and a resident of Perry county; private Virginia Militia; enrolled on December 18, 1833, under act of Congress of June 7, 1832, payment to date from March 4, 1831; annual allowance, $32; sums received to date of publication of list, $96.—*Revolutionary Pension Roll*, in Vol. xiv, Sen. Doc. 514, 23rd Cong., 1st sess., 1833-34.

MAYFIELD, SAMUEL, aged 75, and a resident of Tuscaloosa county; private S. C. Militia; enrolled on April 18, 1833, under act of Congress of June 7, 1832, payment to date from March 4, 1831; annual allowance, $26.66.—*Revolutionary Pension Roll*, in Vol. xiv, Sen. Doc. 514, 23rd Cong., 1st sess., 1833-34.

MAYRANT, JOHN, lieutenant in the navy, particular service not shown; annual allowance, $360; to be paid from September, 1835; transferred from South Carolina.—*Pension Book,* State Branch Bank, Mobile.

MELAM, JOHN, aged 81, and a resident of Madison county; private Virginia Continental Line; enrolled on December 31, 1832, under act of Congress of June 7, 1832, payment to date from March 4, 1831; annual allowance, $80.—*Revolutionary Pension Roll,* in Vol. xiv, 23rd Cong., 1st sess., 1833-34.

MEREDITH, JESSE, aged 79, and a resident of Dallas county; private Virginia Continental Line; enrolled on November 10, 1819, under act of Congress of March 18, 1818, payment to date from September 27, 1819; annual allowance, $96; sums received to date of publication of list, $1,008. Suspended under act May 1, 1820. Continued from March 4, 1823, and transferred from Smith county, Tennessee.—*Revolutionary Pension Roll,* in Vol. xiv, Sen. Doc. 514, 23rd Cong., 1st sess., 1833-34.

MERRICK, JOHN, sen., aged 82, resided in Dale county, June 1, 1840.—*Census of Pensioners,* 1841, p. 149.

MILLARD, NATHANIEL, age not given, a resident of Dallas county; private Tennessee Militia; enrolled on January 15, 1823; payment to date from Sept. 1, 1822; annual allowance, $48; sums received to date of publication of list, $430.31; Acts military Establishment.—*Revolutionary Pension Roll,* in Vol. xiv, Sen. Doc. 514, 23rd Cong., 1st sess., 1833-34.

MILLER, LEONARD, aged 80, and a resident of Jefferson county; private N. C. Continental Line; enrolled on September 26, 1833, under act of Congress of June 7, 1832, payment to date from March 4, 1831; annual allowance, $20; sums received to date of publication of list, $50.—*Revolutionary Pension Roll,* in Vol. xiv, Sen. Doc. 514, 23rd Cong., 1st sess., 1833-34.

MILLER, SAMUEL, age not given, a resident of Franklin county; private 39th Regular U. S. Infantry; enrolled on March 10, 1818; payment to date from July 9, 1814; annual allowance, $96; sums received to date of publication of list, $1,887.09; April 24, 1816, transferred from West Tennessee from September 4, 1819.—*Revolutionary Pension Roll,* in Vol. xiv, Sen. Doc. 514, 23rd Cong., 1st sess., 1833-34.

MILLS, MORGAN, age not given, a resident of Dallas county; private 2nd Regulars New Jersey Line; enrolled on

Revolutionary Soldiers in Alabama. 85

December 18, 1828, under act of Congress of May 15, 1828, payment to date from March 3, 1826; annual allowance, $80; sums received to date of publication of list, $680.—*Revolutionary Pension Roll,* in Vol. xiv, Sen. Doc. 514, 23rd Cong., 1st sess., 1833-34. He resided in Dallas county, June 1, 1840, aged 78.—*Census of Pensioners,* 1841, p. 149.

MITCHELL, FLUD, aged 77, and a resident of Limestone county; private and sergeant N. C. Militia; enrolled on February 21, 1833, under act of Congress of June 7, 1832, payment to date from March 4, 1831; annual allowance, $80; sums received to date of publication of list, $240.—*Revolutionary Pension Roll,* in Vol. xiv, Sen. Doc. 514, 23rd Cong., 1st sess., 1833-34.

MITCHELL, JACOB, a resident of Montgomery county; private, particular service not shown; enrolled on November 21, 1829, under act of Congress of March 18, 1818, payment to date from September 4, 1835; annual allowance, $96.—*Pension Book,* State Branch Bank, Mobile.

MITCHELL, JESSE, aged 75, and a resident of Limestone county; private and sergeant; enrolled on February 23, 1833, under act of Congress of June 7, 1832, payment to date from March 4, 1831; annual allowance, $80; sums received to date of publication of list, $200.—*Revolutionary Pension Roll,* in Vol. xiv, Sen. Doc. 514, 23rd Cong., 1st sess., 1833-34. He resided in Limestone county, June 1, 1840, aged 75.—*Census of Pensioners,* 1841, p. 148.

MITCHELL, WILLIAM, aged 78, and a resident of Morgan county; private Virginia Continental Line; enrolled on July 28, 1824, under act of Congress of March 18, 1818, payment to date from April 26, 1824; annual allowance, $96; sums received to date of publication of list, $802.39.—*Revolutionary Pension Roll,* in Vol. xiv, Sen. Doc. 514, 23rd Cong., 1st sess., 1833-34. He resided in Lawrence county, June 1, 1840, with A. Mitchell, aged 86.—*Census of Pensioners,* 1841, p. 148.

MOND, DUNCAN, private, particular service not shown; annual allowance, $48; records do not show that any payment was made.—*Pension Book,* State Branch Bank, Mobile.

MOORE, OBADIAH, aged 80, and a resident of Autauga county; private N. C. Militia; enrolled on January 4, 1833, under act of Congress of June 7, 1832, payment to date from March 4, 1831; annual allowance, $20; sums received to date of publication of list, $60.—*Revolutionary Pension Roll*, in Part 3, Vol. xiii, Sen. Doc. 514, 23rd Cong., 1st sess., 1833-34.

MORGAN, ASA, aged 74, and a resident of Limestone county; sergeant and private Georgia Militia; enrolled on August 12, 1833, under act of Congress of June 7, 1832; payment to date from March 4, 1831; annual allowance, $83.91; sums received to date of publication of list, $209.77.—*Revolutionary Pension Roll*, in Vol. xiv, Sen. Doc. 514, 23rd Cong., 1st sess., 1833-34.

MORGAN, DANIEL, private and sergeant, particular service not shown; annual allowance, $100; records show that he was paid up to March 4, 1834.—*Pension Book*, State Branch Bank, Mobile.

MORGAN, JAMES, aged 75, and a resident of Perry county; private N. C. Militia; enrolled on September 17, 1833, under act of Congress of June 7, 1832; payment to date from March 4, 1831; annual allowance, $30; sums received to date of publication of list, $75.—*Revolutionary Pension Roll*, in Vol. xiv, Sen. Doc. 514, 23rd Cong., 1st sess., 1833-34.

MORGAN, JOHN, aged 71, and a resident of Fayette county; private N. C. Militia; enrolled on January 31, 1834, under act of Congress of June 7, 1832, payment to date from March 4, 1831; annual allowance, $60; sums received to date of publication of list, $180.—*Revolutionary Pension Roll*, in Vol. xiv, Sen. Doc. 514, 23rd Cong., 1st sess., 1833-34.

MORRIS, ISAAC, aged 74, and a resident of Perry county; sergeant Virginia Militia; enrolled on October 3, 1833, under act of Congress of June 7, 1832, payment to date from March 4, 1831; annual allowance, $40; sums received to date of publication of list, $120.—*Revolutionary Pension Roll*, in Vol. xiv, Sen. Doc. 514, 23rd Cong., 1st sess., 1833-34.

MORRIS, JOHN, aged 70, and a resident of Jackson county; private S. C. State Troops; enrolled on August 12, 1833, under act of Congress of June 7, 1832, payment to date from March 4, 1831; annual allowance, $20; sums received to date of publication of list, $60.—*Revolutionary Pension Roll*, in Vol. xiv, Sen. Doc. 514, 23rd Cong., 1st sess., 1833-34. He resided in Jackson county, June 1, 1840, aged 76.—*Census of Pensioners*, 1841, p. 148.

MORROW, DAVID, aged 71, and a resident of Lawrence county; private of cavalry S. C. Militia; enrolled on December 18, 1833, under act of Congress of June 7, 1832, payment to date from March 4, 1831; annual allowance, $85; sums received to date of publication of list, $215.—*Revolutionary Pension Roll,* in Vol. xiv, Sen. Doc. 514, 23rd Cong., 1st sess., 1833-34.

MORROW, HUGH, a resident of Jefferson county; private, particular service not shown; enrolled on March 15, 1833, under act of Congress of June 7, 1832, payment to date from September 4, 1833; annual allowance, $20.—*Pension Book,* State Branch Bank, Mobile.

MORROW, SAMUEL, aged 88, and a resident of Fayette county; private S. C. Continental Line; enrolled on November 5, 1833, under act of Congress of June 7, 1832, payment to date from March 4, 1831; annual allowance, $45.77; sums received to date of publication of list, $137.31.—*Revolutionary Pension Roll,* in Vol. xiv, Sen. Doc. 514, 23rd Cong., 1st sess., 1833-34.

MOSS, E., aged 74, resided in Cherokee county, June 1, 1840.—*Census of Pensioners,* 1841, p. 148.

MULLINS, STEPHEN, aged 74, and a resident of Blount county; dragoon Virginia Continental Line; enrolled on April 23, 1833, under act of Congress of June 7, 1832, payment to date from March 4, 1831; annual allowance, $100; sums received to date of publication of list, $250.—*Revolutionary Pension Roll,* in Part 3, Vol. xiii, Sen. Doc. 514, 1st sess., 1833-34.

MURRAY, DAVID, was born in 1760, and is buried in Talladega county. The tombstone bears the following inscription:

To the memory of
DAVID MURRAY,
a Revolutionary soldier, who
departed this life 8th day
November, 1840, in the 80th
year of his age.

He came from Prince Edward county, Virginia, just after the war and settled in Wilkes county, Georgia. He left several children, among others Hon. Thomas W. Murray, the oldest son, who was born in Lincoln county, Ga., in 1790, and became a man of distinction, being a candidate for Congress when he died. Murray county, Georgia, is named in honor of him.—White's *Statistics of Georgia.*

"It is shown by the records in Washington, D. C., that one David Murray served as a private in Captain Satterlee's company, Colonel Moses Hazen's regiment, Continental troops, Revolutionary War. He enlisted December 30, 1776; was taken prisoner August 27, ——, and returned to his company August 4, 1779. His name last appears as that of a private on a roll, not dated, 'of Persons in the Congress' Own Regt. commanded by Col. Moses Hazen, Brig. Genl. by Brevet in the service of the U. S., 1783,' with remarks: 'When commissioned or enlisted, 30 Dec., 1776; How Long to Serve, War, 1 year; Discharged by Commander-in-Chief at close of war, 17 June, 1783.' "—Mrs. P. H. Mell in *Transactions* of the Alabama Historical Society, Vol. iv, pp. 556-557.

MURRAY, JAMES, a resident of Perry county, and later of Pickens; private, particular service not shown; enrolled on March 6, 1833, under act of Congress of June 7, 1832, payment to date from September 4, 1833; annual allowance, $80.66.—*Pension Book,* State Branch Bank, Mobile.

NAIL, MATTHEW, aged 77, and a resident of Madison county; private Georgia Militia; enrolled on November 4, 1833, under act of Congress of June 7, 1832, payment to date from March 4, 1831; annual allowance, $80; sums received to date of publication of list, $240.—*Revolutionary Pension Roll,* in Vol. xiv, Sen. Doc. 514, 23rd Cong., 1st sess., 1833-34.

NEELY, JOHN, a resident of Shelby county; private, particular service not shown; enrolled on April 2, 1836, under act of Congress of June 7, 1832, payment to date from March 4, 1831; annual allowance, $20.—*Pension Book,* State Branch Bank, Mobile.

NEIL, ROBERT, age not given, a resident of Greene county; corporal in Mencon's Regiment; enrolled on June 10, 1817, payment to date from March 5, 1814; annual allowance, $60; sums received, $128.30; on April 24, 1816, rate increased to annual allowance of $96, under which the sum of $850.89 received; under act of March 3, 1819, to date from March 4, 1825, rate reduced to annual allowance of $64, under which $576 received to date of publication of list.—*Revolutionary Pension Roll,* in Vol. xiv, Sen. Doc. 514, 23rd Cong., 1st sess., 1833-34.

NELSON, ANDREW, aged 72, and a resident of Morgan county; private Virginia Continental Line; enrolled on July 2, 1833, under act of Congress of June 7, 1832, payment to date from March 4, 1831; annual allowance, $35.44; sums received to date of publication of list, $106.32.—*Revolutionary Pension*

Revolutionary Soldiers in Alabama.   89

Roll, in Vol. xiv, Sen. Doc. 514, 23rd Cong., 1st sess., 1833-34. He resided in Walker county, June 1, 1840, with Robert Howard, aged 76.—*Census of Pensioners,* 1841, p. 150.

NELSON, JOSEPH, aged 77, and a resident of Madison county; private Virginia Continental Line; enrolled on January 22, 1843, under act of Congress of June 7, 1832, payment to date from March 4, 1831; annual allowance, $30; sums received to date of publication of list, $90.—*Revolutionary Pension Roll,* in Vol. xiv, Sen. Doc. 514, 23rd Cong., 1st sess., 1833-34. He resided in Morgan county, June 1, 1840, aged 87.—*Census of Pensioners,* 1841, p. 148.

NEWSOM, RANDOLPH, aged 76, and a resident of Tuscaloosa county; musician N. C. Militia; enrolled on October 29, 1833, under act of Congress of June 7, 1832, payment to date from March 4, 1831; annual allowance, $88; sums received to date of publication of list, $220.—*Revolutionary Pension Roll,* in Vol. xiv, Sen. Doc. 514, 23rd Cong., 1st sess., 1833-34.

NICHOLSON, HARRISON. The grave of this soldier is in the cemetery in Tuskegee. This is the inscription upon his monument:

In memory of
HARRISON NICHOLSON,
A Revolutionary Soldier,
Who was born on the 12th
day of March, A. D. 1760,
and departed this life
on the 28th day of June, 1841,
Aged 81 years, 3 months,
and 16 days.

"The descendants of Harrison Nicholson do not know where he was born or what State claimed him as a soldier during the Revolution. He came from Georgia, near Milledgeville, to Macon county, Ala. He married Lucinda Long Dec. 30, 1783. He died in Macon county at the home of his grandson, James Monroe Nicholson. According to the recollection of his granddaughter, Mrs. E. A. Wilkinson, he had only three sons: (1) Britton Nicholson lived to mature years, but never married; (2) Nathaniel Nicholson married and raised a family; he lived in Georgia in the vicinity of Milledgeville on his plantation; (3) James Nicholson, born March 18, 1785, married Mary M. Stone, October 7th, 1813; children: 1, Mathew H. Nicholson, born Jan. 7th, 1815, married Miss H. E. Savory,

December 9th, 1839, in Mexico, lived there for several years, then moved to Texas, California and to Central America, where he died. His children are now living around Chapel Hill, Texas; 2. Washington B. Nicholson, born June 28, 1818, married in Macon county, Alabama, to Miss Wafer, later moved to Claiborne Parish, Louisiana, died there in 1901. His family now live around Baton Rouge; he was the father of Col. James Nicholson, former president of the University of Louisiana at Baton Rouge; 3. Elizabeth Ann Nicholson, born October 25, 1829, married B. R. Taylor, December, 1836; he died leaving one child, Mrs. E. A. Hall, of Autaugaville. She married a second time J. B. Wilkinson, January 12, 1843, by this marriage were born nine children; 4. Lucinda Long Nicholson, born January 23, 1823, married Leonidas Howard and lived at Mulberry, Autauga county, Alabama; there were two living sons and one daughter by this marriage; 5. James Monroe Nicholson, born December 12, 1825, married Rebecca Slaton, children died, second marriage no children, third marriage in Texas, where he is still living near Chapel Hill; 6. Absalom H. Nicholson, born August 30, 1837, never married, was physician, moved to Louisiana, but died in Macon county, Alabama, 1855; and 7. John Wesley Nicholson, born October 2, 1829, died unmarried in 1851, near Autaugaville, had just graduated from Emory College, Georgia."—Mrs. P. H. Mell, in *Transactions* of the Alabama Historical Society, Vol. iv, pp. 557-558.

NICKOL, WILLIAM, aged 69, and a resident of Lawrence county; private of dragoons N. C. Militia; enrolled on April 23, 1833, under act of Congress of June 7, 1832, payment to date from March 4, 1831; annual allowance, $43.33; sums received to date of publication of list, $108.32.—*Revolutionary Pension Roll*, in Vol. xiv, 23rd Cong., 1st sess., 1833-34.

NORRIS, PATRICK, aged 72, and a resident of Greene county; private S. C. Militia; enrolled on September 28, 1833, under act of Congress of June 7, 1832, payment to date from March 4, 1831; annual allowance, $80; sums received to date of publication of list, $200.—*Revolutionary Pension Roll*, Vol. xiv, Sen. Doc. 514, 23rd Cong., 1st sess., 1833-34.

OAKS, ISAAC, aged 74, and a resident of Perry county; private Virginia Militia; enrolled on October 29, 1833, under act of Congress of June 7, 1832, payment to date from March 4, 1831; annual allowance, $60; sums received to date of publication of list, $150.—*Revolutionary Pension Roll*, in Vol. xiv,

Revolutionary Soldiers in Alabama. 91

Sen. Doc. 514, 23rd Cong., 1st sess., 1833-34. He resided in Perry county, June 1, 1840, with Willis Osbourn, aged 81.—*Census of Pensioners,* 1841, p. 149.

ODOM, JACOB, aged 72, and a resident of Pickens county; private N. C. Militia; enrolled on January 28, 1833, under act of Congress of June 7, 1832, payment to date from March 4, 1831; annual allowance, $20; sums received to date of publication of list, $50.—*Revolutionary Pension Roll,* in Vol. xiv, Sen. Doc. 514, 23rd Cong., 1st sess., 1833-34.

OLIVER, THOMAS. "The writer has been told that the grave of this soldier may be seen near one of the public roads about six miles from Montgomery. His tombstone relates that he was in the War of the Revolution from Culpepper county, Virginia; he was at King's Mountain and Yorktown. He died in 182-- in Montgomery county, Alabama. Nothing more has been learned of his history or family."—Mrs. P. H. Mell in *Transactions* of the Alabama Historical Society, Vol. iv, p. 558.

OSTEEN, DAVID, aged 73, and a resident of Morgan county; private N. C. Militia; enrolled on May 2, 1833, under act of Congress of June 7, 1832, payment to date from March 4, 1831; annual allowance, $23.33; sums received to date of publication of list, $69.99.—*Revolutionary Pension Roll,* in Vol. xiv, Sen. Doc. 514, 23rd Cong., 1st sess., 1833-34.

OTTERSON, SAMUEL, aged 80, and a resident of Greene county; captain and major S. C. Militia; enrolled on July 2, 1833, under act of Congress of June 7, 1832, payment to date from March 4, 1831; annual allowance, $525; sums received to date of publication of list, $1,585.—*Revolutionary Pension Roll,* in Vol. xiv, Sen. Doc. 514, 23rd Cong., 1st sess., 1833-34.

OTTERSON, SAMUEL, age not given, and a resident of Greene county; captain S. C. Militia; date enrolled not stated, but pension to date from Oct. 6, 1816, under act of Congress, March 3, 1809; transferred from S. C., March 4, 1834; annual allowance, $96; sums received to date of publication of list, $2,247.74.—*Revolutionary Pension Roll,* in Vol. xiv, Sen. Doc. 514, 23rd Cong., 1st sess., 1833-34.

OWEN, JOHN, a resident of Autauga county; private, particular service not shown; enrolled on January 26, 1835, under act of Congress of June 7, 1832, payment to date from March 4, 1831; annual allowance, $26.66.—*Pension Book,* State Branch Bank, Mobile.

OWEN, RICHARDSON. "At his residence in Tuscaloosa, Ala., on the 24th day of July, 1822, departed this life Col. Richardson Owen in the 78th year of his life. Col. Owen was born in Henrico county, Virginia, on the 14th of March, 1744. He emigrated to N. Carolina in 1762, where he was appointed Col. Commandant of Randolph county. During the period of the Revolutionary War he retained this command and was for some time in active service. He participated in many of the interesting and painful events with the Revolution. Near the close of the War he resigned this command and removed to Va. on New River where he found a brisk partisan war kept up between Whigs and Tories.

"Devoted to the cause of liberty, he could not remain neutral in this conflict. The Tory party for a while appeared dominant and Col. Owen was selected as one of the victims of their cruelty; his vigilance and activity, however, enabled him to elude their grasp, but his whole estate (which was large) was swept away by them. They burned his house and plundered him of everything movable. Fired by patriotic feelings as well as individual resentment Col. Owen determined at once to crush this murderous band of unprincipled desperadoes. For this purpose he raised a volunteer regiment whom he commanded, and after many sharp conflicts he succeeded in killing, hanging and putting to flight these destroyers of his fortune and enemies of his country's liberties. He carried with him to the grave all those feelings which animated the American soldier in the times that tried men's souls.

"Though he encountered many privations and sustained losses which he was ever after unable to repair, still he felt himself amply compensated in the acquisitions of that liberty for which he fought and struggled and which he long lived to enjoy.

"Nature endowed him with a strong mind, which he retained to the close of his life. In his deportment through life his conduct was exemplary. For more than 20 years he was a member of the Methodist church and daily engaged in the pious duties of a Christian.

"He faced death with confidence and without fear, leaving an aged wife, five sons and one daughter."—Obituary, written by Col. John I. Inge, Tuscaloosa, Ala., and published in the *Tuscaloosa Republican*, July, 1822.

PAINE, MATHEW, age not given, a resident of Marion county; private Tennessee Volunteers; enrolled on February 3, 1826, payment to date from October 26, 1825; annual allow-

Revolutionary Soldiers in Alabama. 93

ance, $96; sums received to date of publication of list, $706.65; April 24, 1816.—*Revolutionary Pension Roll,* in Vol. xiv, Sen. Doc. 514, 23rd Cong., 1st sess., 1833-34.

PARKER, ELISHA. "Departed this life in Morgan county, Ala., on the 21st ult., ELISHA PARKER, in the 97th year of his age, a native of Connecticut, and a soldier of the Revolution. He was greatly esteemed and respected by all who knew him."—*The Democrat,* Huntsville, May 6, 1846.

PARKER, WILLIAM, age not given, a resident of Madison county; private 4th Regular U. S. Infantry; enrolled on September 6, 1820, payment to date from March 11, 1819; annual allowance, $96; sums received to date of publication of list, $1,437.90; Acts Military establishment.—*Revolutionary Pension Roll,* in Vol. xiv, Sen. Doc. 514, 23rd Cong., 1st sess., 1833-34.

PARR, JOHN. "DIED, on the 6th inst., at his residence about eight miles west of this place, Mr. John Parr, in the eigthy-seventh year of his age.

"Mr. Parr emigrated from Fairfield District, S. Carolina, to this State about twelve years ago, and has since resided in the county till his death.

"He entered into the service of his country at the age of sixteen, in the Revolutionary war, and served two campaigns. No man has left behind him a more unblemished character."—*Alabama Beacon,* Greensboro, Ala., January 16, 1847.

PAYNE, MATHEY, aged 76, resided in Walker county, June 1, 1840.—*Census of Pensioners,* 1841, p. 150.

PAYNE, WILLIAM, a resident of Marengo county; private, particular service not shown; enrolled on March 13, 1835, under act of Congress of June 7, 1832, payment to date from March 4, 1831; annual allowance, $20.—*Pension Book,* State Branch Bank, Mobile.

PENDEGRASS, SPENCER, aged 69, resided in Talladega county, June 1, 1840.—*Census of Pensioners,* 1841, p. 148.

PENN, STEPHEN, aged 74, and a resident of Lawrence county; private Maryland State Troops; enrolled on May 2, 1833, under act of Congress of June 7, 1832, payment to date from March 4, 1831; annual allowance, $31.33.—*Revolutionary Pension Roll,* in Vol. xiv, Sen. Doc. 514, 23rd Cong., 1st sess., 1833-34.

PERRY, ABRAHAM, aged 69, and a resident of Butler county; private S. C. Militia; enrolled October 3, 1833, under act of Congress of June 7, 1832, payment to date from March 4, 1831; annual allowance, $80; sums received to date of publication of list, $200.—*Revolutionary Pension Roll*, in Part 3, Vol. xiii, Sen. Doc. 514, 23rd Cong., 1st sess., 1833-34.

PETTIGREW, JAMES, aged 73, and a resident of Greene county; private S. C. Militia; enrolled on July 2, 1833, under act of Congress of June 7, 1832, payment to date from March 4, 1831; annual allowance, $80; sums received to date of publication of list, $240.—*Revolutionary Pension Roll*, in Vol. xiv, Sen. Doc. 514, 23rd Cong., 1st sess., 1833-34. He resided in Greene county, June 1, 1840, aged 79.—*Census of Pensioners*, 1841, p. 149.

PETTY, THEOPHILUS, sen., aged 82, resided in Butler county, June 1, 1840.—*Census of Pensioners*, 1841, p. 149.

PETTY, WILLIAM, aged 70, and a resident of Madison county; private N. C. Militia; enrolled on February 21, 1833, under act of Congress of June 7, 1832, payment to date from March 4, 1831; annual allowance, $20; sums received to date of publication of list, $50.—*Revolutionary Pension Roll*, in Vol. xiv, Sen. Doc. 514, 23rd Cong., 1st sess., 1833-34.

PHILLIPS, ANDREW, aged 75, and a resident of Pickens county; private N. C. Continental Line; enrolled on July 2, 1833, under act of Congress of June 7, 1832, payment to date from March 4, 1831; annual allowance, $80.—*Revolutionary Pension Roll*, in Vol. xiv, Sen. Doc. 514, 23rd Cong., 1st sess., 1833-34.

PIERCE, HUGH, a resident of Jefferson county; private, particular service not shown; enrolled on Septembr 17, 1834, under act of Congress of June 7, 1832, payment to date from March 4, 1831; annual allowance, $30.—*Pension Book*, State Branch Bank, Mobile.

PIERCE, JOHN, aged 82, and a resident of Dallas county; private S. C. Militia; enrolled on March 5, 1833, under act of Congress of June 7, 1832, payment to date from March 4, 1831; annual allowance, $40; sums received to date of publication of list, $120.—*Revolutionary Pension Roll*, in Vol. xiv, Sen. Doc. 514, 23rd Cong., 1st sess., 1833-34. He resided in Dallas county, June 1, 1840, with Benjamin Crumblin, aged 95.—*Census of Pensioners*, 1841, p. 149.

PIGG, CHARLES, aged 70, and a resident of Madison county; private Virginia Continental Line; enrolled on December 31, 1832, under act of Congress of June 7, 1832, payment to date from March 4, 1831; annual allowance, $20; sums received to date of publication of list, $60.—*Revolutionary Pension Roll,* in Vol. xiv, Sen. Doc. 514, 23rd Cong., 1st sess., 1833-34.

POOL, JOHN, aged 74, and a resident of Perry county; private S. C. Militia; enrolled on June 5, 1833, under act of Congress of June 7, 1832, payment to date from March 4, 1831; annual allowance, $20; sums received to date of publication of list, $50.—*Revolutionary Pension Roll,* in Vol. xiv, Sen. Doc. 514, 23rd Cong., 1st sess., 1833-34.

POOL, SAMUEL, aged 80, resided in Russell county, June 1, 1840, with Matthew Pool.—*Census of Pensioners,* 1841, p. 149.

POPE, LE ROY. "One by one of those whose good fortune it was to be engaged in the struggle for American Independence quietly drop into the grave. Soon we will have only their memories and the recollection of their achievements to remind us of their patriotic labors.

Col. LE ROY POPE has been gathered to his fathers. For four-score years he led a life singular for its uniform probity and morality. He was born in Virginia in 1764—removed to Georgia in 1790—to this place in 1810, where he resided up to the time of his death on the 14th inst., beloved by his relatives and intimate friends, honored and esteemed by all. He was no common man, possessed of no common mind, and filled no common place in our Society. The bustling incidents of his youth prevented his receiving a complete education; but his mind was one of a strong and vigorous character; bold, original and comprehensive, with a vast fund of common sense. Formerly possessing the whole of the present site of Huntsville, he was looked upon and was one of the chief patrons and founders of the place, and always took a deep interest in whatever affected the welfare of the town. His liberality and benevolence were notorious. The last ten years of his life were spent mostly in retirement, mingling but little in the turmoil of every-day life—preparing in peace, in quiet serenity for another and different world, and at the time of his death he was a leading member of the Episcopal church.

One of the chief pleasures of life, is to sit at the feet of the pioneers of our town and listen to them relate the early history of the place—the incidents connected with its settlement, and its original inhabitants. Acting a conspicuous part in all, and acquainted with all, it was a rare enjoyment to hear Col.

Pope discourse in his colloquial manner of events in our history; and the only regret is that the pleasure was so seldom enjoyed. A mere child to him, a comparative stranger to his many virtues, and the part he acted in life's drama, we cannot speak more at length and with definiteness. His death has created a chasm, an aching void in society, which we know not who can fill.

The action of the mayor and aldermen upon the loss our town has sustained, will be found below.

At a called meeting of the Board of Aldermen of the Town of Huntsville, it was unanimously resolved that the corporate authorities attend the funeral of the late Col. *Le Roy Pope* in token of respect for the many private virtues and public services of the deceased."

June 14th, 1844.—*Southern Advocate,* Huntsville, June 21, 1844.

PORTER, JAMES, age not given, a resident of Dallas county; service and date of enrollment not given because of the loss of papers by the burning of the office of the War Department, 1801 and 1814; payment to date from September 5, 1808; annual allowance, $24, under which the sum of $177.17 received; transferred from Iredell county, N. C., from September 4, 1824; on April 30, 1816, to date from Jan. 22, 1816, rate increased to annual allowance of $48, under which the total sum of $733.82 received; and "on account of increased disability," rate increased, to date from May 4, 1831, to annual allowance of $96, under which the sum of $272.27 received to date of publication of list.—*Revolutionary Pension Roll,* in Vol. xiv, Sen. Doc. 514, 23rd Cong., 1st sess., 1833-34. He resided in Dallas county, June 1, 1840, aged 80.—*Census of Pensioners,* 1841, p. 149.

POSEY, HEZEKIAH, aged 90, resided in Benton county, June 1, 1840.—*Census of Pensioners,* 1841, p. 148.

POWELL, PEYTON, a resident of Madison county; lieutenant First Regular Virginia Line; enrolled on August 29, 1828, under act of Congress of May 15, 1828, payment to date from March 3, 1826; annual allowance, $320; sums received to date of publication of list, $2,720; Lemuel Mead, agent.— *Revolutionary Pension Roll,* in Vol. xiv, Sen. Doc. 514, 23rd Cong., 1st sess., 1833-34. He resided in Madison county, June 1, 1840, aged 80.—*Census of Pensioners,* 1841, p. 148.

PRIDDY, RICHARD, aged 74, and a resident of Morgan county; sergeant Virginia Continental Line; enrolled on June

Revolutionary Soldiers in Alabama. 97

4, 1818, under act of Congress of March 18, 1818, payment to date from May 13, 1818; annual allowance, $96; sums received to date of publication of list, $1,228.90.—*Revolutionary Pension Roll,* in Vol. xiv, Sen. Doc. 514, 23rd Cong., 1st sess., 1833-34.

PRIDE, BURTON, aged 77, and a resident of Morgan county; private Virginia Militia; enrolled on July 2, 1833, under act of Congress of June 7, 1832, payment to date from March 4, 1831; annual allowance, $60; sums received to date of publication of list, $150.—*Revolutionary Pension Roll,* in Vol. xiv, Sen. Doc. 514, 23rd Cong., 1st sess., 1833-34.

PULLEN, WILLIAM, aged 76, and a resident of Jefferson county; private Virginia Continental Line; enrolled on April 12, 1831, under act of Congress of March 18, 1818, payment to date from March 4, 1831; annual allowance, $96; sums received to date of publication of list, $240.—*Revolutionary Pension Roll,* in Vol. xiv, Sen. Doc. 514, 23rd Cong., 1st sess., 1833-34. He resided in Jefferson county, June 1, 1840, aged 82.—*Census of Pensioners,* 1841, p. 149.

"The grave of William Pullen is in Jefferson county, in the suburbs of Birmingham, in an old family burying ground about fifty yards from the Avondale car line between 34th and 35th streets. For many years this old graveyard was as isolated and secluded as if situated in the heart of a lonely forest, but, in the last year or two, houses have been built up thickly around it and are encroaching upon its boundaries. The grave of the soldier lies at the foot of a large oak tree; it is a rough mound of brown stones with a flat tablet topping them which bears this inscription:

Sacred to the
Memory of
WILLIAM PULLEN
A Soldier of the
Revolution,
Who died April 4th, 1845,
Aged 87 years.

"His wife lies at his feet but the lettering of the tablet at her grave is illegible, only the words 'Wife of William Pullen.'

"Descendants of William Pullen declare that he died at the age of ninety-six and that he was born in the year 1749. But as his name is found in the *Census of Pensioners* for 1840 and he is recorded as being eighty-two years of age at that date, and this agrees perfectly with what appears to be the age on the tombstone, the writer has accepted the latter as correct. William Pullen then was born in Virginia in 1758, on the Appomattox river near Petersburg. He entered the Revolutionary War from Virginia and was in service for seven years. Soon after the Revolution he moved to South Carolina and in 1820 he came to Alabama and settled near Birmingham. He was the first man buried with military honors in Jefferson county.

"He left six children: (1) Clarissa, who married Jesse Hickman, and they were the parents of W. P. Hickman, formerly county commissioner for Jefferson county; (2) Sarah who married James Rowan, and they were the parents of Peyton Rowan, of Jacksonville, Ala.; (3) William, married Nancy Brooks; (4) Martha, married Joseph Hickman; (5) Mary, married Samuel Rowan; (6) Elizabeth, married Richard Tankersley.

"It is shown in the records at Washington, D. C., in the Record and Pension Office, 'that one William Pullen served as a private in Captain George Lambert's company of Continental regulars of the 14th battalion, 14th Virginia regiment of foot, commanded by Colonel Charles Lewis, Revolutionary War.' He enlisted January 1, 1777, to serve three years, a: his name last appears as that of a private on a roll dateu Camp near Morristown, December 9, 1779, of Captain Overton's company, 10th Virginia regiment, commanded by Col. William Davies. The records show that the 14th Virginia Regiment became the 10th Virginia regiment about November, 1778, and that about May, 1779, the 1st and 10th Virginia regiments were incorporated and designated the 1st and 10th Virginia regiment."—Mrs. P. H. Mell, in *Transactions* of the Alabama Historical Society, Vol. iv, pp. 558-560.

QUEEN, THOMAS, aged 82, and a resident of Morgan county; private N. C. Militia; enrolled on July 2, 1833, under act of Congress of June 7, 1832, payment to date from March 4, 1831; annual allowance, $55; sums received to date of publication of list, $165.—*Revolutionary Pension Roll*, in Vol. xiv, Sen. Doc. 514, 23rd Cong., 1st Sess., 1833-34. He resided in Morgan county, June 1, 1840, aged 80.—*Census of Pensioners*, 1841, p. 148.

QUINN, MICHAEL, private, particular service not shown; annual allowance, $96; transferred to South Carolina.—*Pension Book*, State Branch Bank, Mobile.

RALEY, CHARLES, aged 70, and a resident of Morgan county; private of Cavalry Virginia Continental Line; enrolled

Revolutionary Soldiers in Alabama. 99

on September 17, 1833, under act of Congress of June 7, 1832, payment to date from March 4, 1831; annual allowance, $77.72; sums received to date of publication of list, $194.30.—*Revolutionary Pension Roll,* in Vol. xiv, Sen. Doc. 514, 23rd Cong., 1st sess., 1833-34.

RANDOLPH, ABRAHAM, aged 72, and a resident of Lawrence county; private N. C. Militia, enrolled on April 13, 1833, under act of Congress of June 7, 1832, payment to date from March 4, 1831; annual allowance, $20.—*Revolutionary Pension Roll,* in Vol. xiv, Sen. Doc. 514, 23rd Cong., 1st sess., 1833-34.

RANDOLPH, HUGH, aged 85, resided in Franklin county, June 1, 1840, with David Fuller.—*Census of Pensioners,* 1841, p. 148.

RANKIN, ROBERT, a resident of Washington county; lieutenant 3rd Regular Virginia Line; enrolled on September 8, 1828, under act of Congress of May 15, 1828, payment to date from March 3, 1826; annual allowance, $320; sums received to date of publication of list, $2,880; W. Crawford, agent.—*Revolutionary Penison Roll,* in Vol. xiv, Sen. Doc. 514, 23rd Cong., 1st sess., 1833-34.

RAY, FREDERICK, aged 75, and a resident of Tuscaloosa county; private Virginia State Troops; enrolled on April 23, 1833, under act of Congress of June 7, 1832, payment to date from March 4, 1831; annual allowance, $36.66.—*Revolutionary Pension Roll,* in Vol. xiv, Sen. Doc. 514, 23rd Cong., 1st sess., 1833-34.

READY, SHADRACK, aged 88, and a resident of Madison county; private Virginia Continental Line; enrolled on December 5, 1820, under act of Congress of March 18, 1818, payment to date from September 11, 1820; annual allowance, $96; sums received to date of publication of list, $438.13. Died April 3, 1825.—*Revolutionary Pension Roll,* in Vol. xiv, Sen. Doc. 514, 23rd Cong., 1st sess., 1833-34.

REED, JOHN. aged 82, and a resident of Fayette county; private N. C. Militia; enrolled on November 15, 1833, under act of Congress of June 7, 1832, payment to date from March 4, 1831; annual allowance, $30; sums received to date of publication of list, $90.—*Revolutionary Pension Roll,* in Vol. xiv, Sen. Doc. 514, 23rd Cong., 1st sess., 1833-34.

REED, NATHAN, aged 72, and a resident of Perry county; private N. C. Militia; enrolled on September 17, 1833, under act of Congress of June 7, 1832, payment to date from March 4, 1831; annual allowance, $30; sums received to date of publication of list, $75.—*Revolutionary Pension Roll,* in Vol. xiv, Sen. Doc. 514, 23rd Cong., 1st sess., 1833-34.

REED, ROBERT, aged 77, and a resident of St. Clair county; private and sergeant N. C. Militia; enrolled on February 4, 1833, under act of Congress of June 7, 1832, payment to date from March 4, 1831; annual allowance, $65; sums received to date of publication of list, $195.—*Revolutionary Pension Roll,* in Vol. xiv, Sen. Doc. 514, 23rd Cong., 1st sess., 1833-34. He resided in St. Clair county, June 1, 1840, aged 75.—*Census of Pensioners,* 1841, p. 148.

REESE, LITTLETON, aged 76, resided in Autauga county, June 1, 1840.—*Census of Pensioners,* 1841, p. 149.

REYNOLDS, FIELDING, aged 70, and a resident of Dallas county; private and sergeant S. C. State Troops; enrolled on March 8, 1833, under act of Congress of June 7, 1832, payment to date from March 4, 1831; annual allowance, $93.33; sums received to date of publication of list, $279.99. —*Revolutionary Pension Roll,* in Vol. xiv, Sen. Doc. 514, 23rd Cong., 1st sess., 1833-34.

RICE, RIGHT, a resident of Wilcox county; private, particular service not shown; enrolled on January 26, 1835, under act of Congress of June 7, 1832, payment to date from March 4, 1831; annual allowance, $20.—*Pension Book,* State Branch Bank, Mobile.

RIDNER, SAMUEL, aged 80, resided in Benton county, June 1, 1840, with Jos. Ridner.—*Census of Pensioners,* 1841, p. 148.

ROANE, JAMES H., age not given, a resident of Morgan county; 2nd lieutenant 10th Regular U. S. Infantry; enrolled on April 18, 1825, payment to date from January 28, 1825; annual allowance, $90; sums received to date of publication of list, $684.22; Acts Military establishment.—*Revolutionary Pension Roll,* in Vol. xiv, Sen. Doc. 514, 23rd Cong., 1st sess., 1833-34.

ROBERSON, JOHN, aged 74, and a resident of Tuscaloosa county; private Virginia Militia; enrolled on July 20, 1833, under act of Congress of June 7, 1832, payment to date from March 4, 1831; annual allowance, $28.11; sums received to date of publication of list, $70.38.—*Revolutionary Pension Roll,* in Vol. xiv, Sen. Doc. 514, 23rd Cong., 1st sess., 1833-34.

ROBERTS, DAVID, aged 89, and a resident of Shelby county; private S. C. Militia; enrolled on March 12, 1834, under act of Congress of June 7, 1832, payment to date from March 4, 1831; annual allowance, $60; sums received to date of publication of list, $180.—*Revolutionary Pension Roll*, in Vol. xiv, Sen. Doc. 514, 23rd Cong., 1st sess., 1833-34.

ROBERTSON, JAMES, aged 71, and a resident of St. Clair county; private S. C. Continental Line; enrolled on October 29, 1833, under act of Congress of June 7, 1832; payment to date from March 4, 1831; annual allowance, $80; sums received to date of publication of list, $240.—*Revolutionary Pension Roll*, in Vol. xiv, Sen. Doc. 514, 23rd Cong., 1st sess., 1833-34.

"The following tribute to 'Horseshoe Robinson' is extracted from a poem, entitled 'The Day of Freedom,' by Alexander B. Meek, and delivered as an oration at Tuscaloosa on the 4th of July, 1838:

"Valoriously
He bore himself, and with his youthful arms
Chivalrous deeds performed, which in a land
Of legendary lore had placed his name,
Embalmed in song, beside the hallowed ones
Of Douglass and of Percy; not unsung
Entirely his fame. Romance has wreathed
With flowering fingers, and with wizard art
That hangs the votive chaplet on the heart,
His story, mid her fictions, and hath given
His name and deeds to after times. When last
This trophied anniversary came round
And called Columbia's patriot children out
To greet its advent, the old man was here,
Serenely smiling as the autumn sun
Just dripping down the golden west to seek
His evening couch. Few months agone I saw
Him in his quiet home, with all around
Its wishes could demand—and by his side
The loved companion of his youthful years—
This singing maiden of his boyhood's time;
She who had cheered him with her smiles when clouds
Were o'er his country's prospects; who had trod
In sun and shade, life's devious path with him,
And whom kind Heaven had still preserved to bless,
With all the fullness of maternal wealth,
The mellowing afternoon of his decline.
Where are they now?—the old man and his wife?
Alas! the broadening sun sets in the night,
The ripening shock falls on the reaper's arm;
The lingering guest must leave the hall at last;
The music ceases when the feast is done;
The old man and his wife are gone. From earth,
Have passed in peace to heaven; and summer's flowers,

> Beneath the light of this triumphant day,
> Luxurious sweets are shedding o'er
> The unsculptured grave of 'Horseshoe Robinson.'"

"The grave of James Robertson is in Tuscaloosa county on the banks of the Black Warrior river near Sanders' ferry, in the old family burying-ground. He was the famous 'Horseshoe Robertson' of Revolutionary fame in South Carolina, and the hero of the novel of that name written by John Pendleton Kennedy in 1835. The name 'Horseshoe' was given because of a bend in a creek in his plantation in South Carolina shaped like a horseshoe.

"The following inscription is taken from his tombstone:

> MAJOR JAMES ROBERTSON,
> A native of S. C.
> died April 26, 1838, aged 79 years,
> and was buried here.
> Well known as Horseshoe Robinson, he earned a
> Just fame in the war of independence, in
> which he was eminent in courage, patriotism
> and suffering. He lived fifty-six years with
> his worthy partner, useful and respected, and
> died in hopes of a blessed immortality. His
> children erect this monument as a tribute
> justly due a good husband, father, neighbor,
> patriot and soldier.

"James Robertson was born in 1759; and his epitaph states that he was a native of South Carolina. He was married in 1782 and 'lived fifty-six years with his worthy partner;' she died in January, 1838, and he died April 26, 1838. The name of his wife was Sarah Morris ——; tradition says her maiden name was Hayden; they left several children, one daughter was living in Mississippi a few years ago. James Robertson was a famous scout during the Revolution and a terror to the Tories. After the war he settled in Pendleton district and was living there when Kennedy met him in 1818. In the preface to Kennedy's novel of *Horseshoe Robinson* he gives an account of the circumstances which led him to write the story.

"He says that in the winter of 1818-19 he had occasion to visit the western section of South Carolina. He went from Augusta to Edgefield, then to Abbeville and thence to Pendleton, in the old district of Ninety-six, just at the foot of the mountains. His course was still westward until he came to the Seneca river, a tributary of the Savannah. He describes how he happened to spend the night at the home of Col. T—, who lived thirty miles from Pendleton . Horseshoe Robinson came here that night. 'What a man I saw! Tall, broad, brawny and erect. His homely dress, his free stride, his face radiant with kindness, the natural gracefulness of his motions, all afforded a ready index to his character. It was evident he was a man to confide in.'

"The old soldier was drawn out to relate some stories of the war. He told how he got away from Charleston after the surrender, and how he took five Scotchmen prisoners, and these two famous passages are faithfully preserved in the narrative.

"It was first published in 1835. Horseshoe Robinson was then a very old man. He had removed to Alabama and lived, I am told, near Tuscaloosa. I commissioned a friend to send him a copy of the book. The report brought me was that the old man had listened very attentively to the reading of it and took great interest in it.

"'What do you say to all this?' was the question addressed to him, after the reading was finished. His reply is a voucher, which I desire to preserve: 'It is all true and right—in its right place—excepting about them women, which I disremember. That mought be true, too; but my memory is treacherous—I disremember.'"

It is a pleasure to know that this fine old hero was a real personage, and although his exploits may have been colored in a measure by the pen of the romancer, there still remains a rich stock of adventures, which were undoubtedly true, and the picture of a nature frank, brave, true and yet full of modesty.

Extract from *Flag of the Union,* published at Tuscaloosa, January 17, 1838:

Horseshoe Robinson—Who has not read Kennedy's delightful novel of this name, and who that has read would not give an half day's ride to see the venerable living Hero of this Tale of "Tory Ascendency," the immortal Horseshoe himself—the extermination of "Jim Curry" and Hugh Habershaw? The venerable patriot bearing the familiar sobriquet, and whose name Mr. Kennedy has made as familiar in the mouths of American youths as household words, was visited by us in company with several friends one day last week. We found the old Gentleman on his Plantation about 12 miles from this city, as comfortably situated with respect to this world's goods as any one could desire to have him. It was gratifying to us to see him in his old age after having served through the whole war of Independence thus seated under his own vine and fig tree, with his children around him and with the Partner of his early toils and trials still continued to him enjoying in peace and safety the rich rewards of that arduous struggle, in the most gloomy and desponding hour of which he was found as ready, as earnest, as zealous, for the cause of liberty as when victory perched upon her standard, and the stars of the "Tory ascendency" was for a while dimmed by defeat—and in which he continued with unshaken Faith and constancy until it sank below the Horison never again to rise. The old gentleman gave us a partial history of his Revolutionary adventures, containing many interesting facts respecting the domination of the Tory party in the South during the times of the Revolution, which Mr. Kennedy has not recorded in his Book. But it will chiefly interest our readers, or to that portion of them at least to whom the history of the old hero's achievements as recorded by Mr. Kennedy is familiar, to be assured that the principal incidents therein portrayed are strictly true.

That of his escape from Charleston after the capture of that city, his being entrusted with a letter to Butler, the scene at Wat Adair's, the capture of Butler at Grindal's Ford, his subsequent escape and recapture, the death of John Ramsey, and the detection of the party by reason of the salute fired over his grave, his capturing of the four men under the common of the younger St. Jermyn, his attack up Ines' camp, and the death of Hugh Habershaw by his own hand and finally the death of Jim Curry, are all narrated pretty much as they occurred, in the old veteran's own language: "There is a heap of truth in it, though the writer has mightily furnished it up." That the names of Butler, Mildred Lindsay, Mary Musgrove, John Ramsay, Hugh Habershaw, Jim Curry and in fact almost every other used in the Book, with the exception of his own, are real and not fictitious. His own name, he informed us, is James; and that he did not go by the familior appellation by which he is now so widely known until after the war, when he acquired it from the form of his Plantation in the Horseshoe Bend of the Fair Forest creek, which was bestowed upon him by the Legislature of South Carolina in consequence of the services he had rendered during the war—this estate, we understood him to say, he still owned.

He was born, he says, in 1759 in Virginia, and entered the army in his seventeenth year. Before the close of war, he says, he commanded a troop of horse, so that his military title is that of Captain. Horseshoe, although in infirm health, bears evident marks of having been a man of great personal strength and activity. He is now afflicted with a troublesome cough, which in the natural course of events must in a few years wear out his aged frame. Yet, notwithstanding his infirmities and general debility, his eye still sparkles with the fire of youth, as he recounts the stirring and thrilling incidents of the war, and that sly, quiet humor so well described by Kennedy may still be seen playing around his mouth as one calls to his recollections any of the pranks he was wont to play upon any of the "tory vagrants," as he very properly styles them. The old Gentleman received us with warm cordiality and hospitality; and after partaking of the Bounties of his board and spending a night under his hospitable roof we took leave of him, sincerely wishing him many years of the peaceful enjoyment of that liberty which he fought so long and so bravely to achieve. It will not be uninteresting, we hope, to remark that the old hero still considers himself a soldier, though the nature of his warfare is changed; he is now a zealous promoter of the Redeemer's cause as he once was in securing the independence of his country.

Since the above was in type we have heard of the death of the aged partner of this venerable patriot. An obituary notice will be found in another column.

Revolutionary Soldiers in Alabama.   105

"The novel *Horseshoe Robinson* is interesting reading even in this critical and blase twentieth century. Judge A. B. Meek, a fine literary critic, says that "Mr. Kennedy, the author of 'Horseshoe Robinson,' has in that inimitable 'Tale of the Tory Ascendency' in South Carolina proved the suitableness of American subjects for fictitious composition of the most elevated kind. Although in his incidents and characters he has done little more than presented a faithful chronicle of facts, using throughout the veritable names of persons and places as they were stated to him by his hero himself, yet such is the thrilling interest of the story, the vivid pictures of scenery, manners, customs, and language, the striking contrasts of characters and the pervading beauty and power of style and description throughout the work, that we think we do not err in saying that it is not inferior in any respect to the best of the Waverly series.'

"The home of James Robertson in South Carolina, where he lived for a third of a century, is still standing. It is in Oconee county a few miles from Westminster. It is now owned by a Mr. Cox and travelers frequently visit the place, drawn thither by the fame of 'Horseshoe Robinson.'"—Mrs. P. H. Mell in *Transactions* of the Alabama Historical Society, Vol. iv, pp. 560-564.

ROBINSON, JOHN, aged 81, resided in Benton county, June 1, 1840, with J. H. Morison.—*Census of Pensioners,* 1841, p. 150.

ROBINSON, WILLIAM, aged 75, and a resident of Montgomery county; private S. C. State Torops; enrolled on January 4, 1834, under act of Congress of June 7, 1832, payment to date from March 4, 1831; annual allowance, $80; sums received to date of publication of list, $240.—*Revolutionary Pension Roll,* in Vol. xiv, Sen. Doc. 514, 23rd Cong., 1st sess., 1833-34.

ROBINSON, WILLIAM, aged 75, and a resident of Autauga county; private S. C. Continental Line and Militia; enrolled on February 11, 1834, under act of Congress of June 7, 1832, payment to date from March 4, 1831; annual allowance, $40.—*Revolutionary Pension Roll,* in Part 3, Vol. xiii, Sen. Doc. 514, 23rd Cong., 1st sess., 1833-34.

RODGERS, JAMES, aged 80, resided in Pickens county, June 1, 1840.—*Census of Pensioners,* 1841, p. 149.

ROGERS, EDWARD, aged 89, and a resident of Tuscaloosa county; private S. C. State Troops; enrolled on August

12, 1833, under act of Congress of June 7, 1832, payment to date from March 4 ,1831; annual allowance, $80; sums received to date of publication of list, $240.—*Revolutionary Pension Roll,* in Vol. xiv, Sen. Doc. 514, 23rd Cong., 1st sess., 1833-34.

ROPER, JOHN, aged 75, resided in Benton county, June 1, 1840, with Stephen Roper.—*Census of Pensioners,* 1841, p. 148.

ROSS, CHARLES, aged 85, and a resident of Morgan county; private Virginia Continental Line; enrolled on May 27, 1824, under act of Congress of March 18, 1818, payment to date from April 26, 1824; annual allowance, $96; sums received to date of publication of list, $670.98.—*Revolutionary Pension Roll,* in Vol. xiv, Sen. Doc. 514, 23rd Cong., 1st sess., 1833-34.

ROSS, WALTER, aged 74, and a resident of Autauga county; private N. C. Militia; enrolled on October 29, 1833, under the act of Congress of June 7, 1832, payment to date from March 4, 1831; annual allowance, $30; sums received to date of publication of list, $90.—*Revolutionary Pension Roll,* in Part 3, Vol. xiii, Sen. Doc. 514, 23rd Cong., 1st sess., 1833-34. He resided in Autauga county, June 1, 1840, aged 81.—*Census of Pensioners,* 1841, p. 149.

ROWAN, SAMUEL, aged 70, and a resident of Jackson county; private S. C. Continental Line ;enrolled on November 22, 1833, under act of Congress of June 7, 1832; payment to date from March 4, 1831; annual allowance, $39.44; sums received to date of publication of list, $118.32.—*Revolutionary Pension Roll,* in Vol. xiv, Sen. Doc. 514, 23rd Cong., 1st sess., 1833-34.

ROWE, JOSHUA, aged 79, resided in Coosa county, June 1, 1840, with Daniel Rowe.—*Census of Pensioners,* 1841, p. 149.

ROWSEY, EDMOND, aged 71, and a resident of Fayette county; private Virginia Militia; enrolled on February 11, 1834, under act of Congress of June 7, 1832, payment to date from March 4, 1831; annual allowance, $20; sums received to date of publication of list, $60.—*Revolutionary Pension Roll,* in Vol. xiv, Sen. Doc. 514, 23rd Cong., 1st sess., 1833-34.

RUSSELL, THOMAS, aged 74, and a resident of Jackson county; private of Cavalry N. C. Continental Line; enrolled on April 22, 1834, under act of Congress of June 7, 1832, pay-

Revolutionary Soldiers in Alabama. 107

ment to date from March 4, 1831; annual allowance, $41.66.—*Revolutionary Pension Roll,* in Vol. xiv, Sen. Doc. 514, 23rd Cong., 1st sess., 1833-34. He resided in Jackson county, June 1, 1840, aged 79.—*Census of Pensioners,* 1841, p. 148.

SAMPELS, JESSE, aged 79, resided in Jackson county, June 1, 1840.—*Census of Pensioners,* 1841, p. 148.

SAMPLE, JOHN, SR., aged 75, and a resident of Marengo county; private S. C. Militia; enrolled on July 25, 1834, under act of Congress of June 7, 1832, payment to date from March 4, 1831; annual allowance, $30.88.—*Revolutionary Pension Roll,* in Vol. xiv, Sen. Doc. 514, 23rd Cong., 1st sess., 1833-34.

SAUNDERS, JOSEPH, aged 77, and a resident of Lawrence county; lieutenant of navy, Virginia State Navy; enrolled on February 14, 1833, under act of Congress of June 7, 1832, payment to date from March 4, 1831; annual allowance, $365.20.—*Revolutionary Pension Roll,* in Vol. xiv, Sen. Doc. 514, 23rd Cong., 1st sess., 1833-34.

SAWYER, STEPHEN, aged 75, and a resident of Greene county; private N. C. Militia; enrolled on March 21, 1834, under act of Congress of June 7, 1832, payment to date from March 4, 1831; annual allowance, $40.—*Revolutionary Pension Roll,* in Vol. xiv, Sen. Doc. 514, 23rd Cong., 1st sess., 1833-34.

SAXON, JAMES, a resident of Autauga county; private, particular service not shown; enrolled on February 16, 1820, under act of Congress of March 18, 1818, payment to date from Septembr 4, 1834; annual allowance, $96; died January 17, 1836.—*Pension Book,* State Branch Bank, Mobile.

SCARBROUGH, ELIAS, aged 94, resided in Clarke county, June 1, 1840.—*Census of Pensioners,* 1841, p. 149.

SEALE, JARVIS, a resident of Greene county; private, particular service not shown; enrolled on July 8, 1835, under act of Congress of June 7, 1832, payment to date from March 4, 1831; annual allowance, $20.—*Pension Book,* State Branch Bank, Mobile.

SEVIER, GOVERNOR JOHN. "This hero of the Revolution, whose life was a romance, was not one of the pioneer settlers of Alabama. He died in this State and his remains lay buried here for seventy-three years 'without a stone to mark the place of their repose or an enclosure to protect them from unhallowed intrusion.' In 1888 his body was removed by the State of Tennessee and laid to rest beneath the sod of the State he had loved and served so faithfully. He is now buried in Knoxvlile, and the State has erected a stately monument as a memorial of her everlasting though tardy gratitude to her honored son.

"Valentine Xavier, the father of John Sevier, was a descendant from an ancient Huguenot family in Navarre; he was born in London and emigrated to America about 1740; settled on the Shenandoah, Virginia; removed to Watauga, N. C., and finally settled on the Nola Chucka, at Plum Grove. —See *Pioneer Women of the West.*

"John Sevier was born in Rockingham Co., Va., 23rd of September, 1745, and was educated at the academy in Fredericksburg. He was married at the early age of seventeen to Sarah Hawkins; soon afterwards he founded Newmarket, in the valley of the Shenandoah; he became at once celebrated as an Indian fighter, and was made captain of the Virginia line in 1772. That spring (1772) he removed to Watauga, now Tennessee, served in Lord Dunmore's war and was in the battle of Point Pleasant, 1774. 'His work began at the dawn of the Revolution and lasted to the end.' It is said he was in thirty battles. His wife's health was delicate and she never removed from Virginia, but died in 1779, leaving him ten children. In 1780, he married Catharine Sherrill, daughter of Samuel Sherrill of North Carolina, who was one of the pioneers in the valley of the Watauga. She was beautiful, tall, strong and courageous as became the wife of John Sevier. She always boasted that the first work she did after she was married was to spin and weave and make the suits of clothes which her husband and his three sons wore in the memorable battle of King's Mountain. She became the mother of eight children, three sons and five daughters. After the battle of King's Mountain, John Sevier received a vote of thanks and a present of a sword and pistol from the North Carolina legislature. A fellow soldier said of his appearance during the battle: 'His eyes were flames of fire, and his words were electric bolts crashing down the ranks of the enemy.'

"He was elected governor of the State of Franklin in 1784; but, as this State was not long allowed existence, Sevier was captured and imprisoned because of alleged disloyalty. However, he was rescued and soon made his escape. That section of country was then given the name by the United States government of 'Territory south of the river Ohio,' and he was made brigadier-general of this section in 1789. He was the first delegate sent to represent the Territory in Congress in 1790. During all this time he was incessantly and successfully engaged in defending the settlements from the Indians until their spirit was broken and peace was fully established. No man was ever more feared or respected by them, and as for the white people of the settlements, they loved him as a father, friend and protector. When the State of Tennessee was established, he was elected the first governor in 1796, and served three terms. In 1815, in spite of his age and infirmities, he was appointed by President Monroe to act as United States commissioner to settle the boundary line between Georgia and the Creek territory in Alabama. He died while engaged in this work, September 24th, 1815. He was attended during his illness by only a few soldiers and Indians. He was buried near Fort Decatur, Alabama, on the east side of the Tallapoosa river, at an Indian village called Tuckabatchee, with the honors of war by the troops under command of Capt. Walker, United States army. He was in the active service of his country from a boy of eighteen until he died at the age of seventy. —Mrs. P. H. Mell in *Transactions* of the Alabama Historical Society, vol. iv, pp. 565-566.

SHEPHERD, R. S., aged 73, resided in Jefferson county, June 1, 1840, with Sarah Nabers.—*Census of Pensioners,* 1841, p. 149.

SHUMAKER, HARMON, aged 73, and a resident of Fayette county; private Maryland Militia; enrolled on July 12, 1834, under act of Congress of June 7, 1832, payment to date from March 4, 1831; annual allowance, $40.—*Revolutionary Pension Roll,* in Vol. xiv, Sen. Doc. 514 ,23rd Cong., 1st sess., 1833-34.

SIBLEY, JOHN, sergeant, particular service not shown; annual allowance, $120; records do not show that any payments were ever made.—*Pension Book,* State Branch Bank, Mobile.

SIMPSON, ELISHA, aged 76, and a resident of Washington county; private N. C. Militia; enrolled on September 24, 1833, under act of Congress of June 7, 1832, payment to date from March 4, 1831; annual allowance, $36.66.—*Revolutionary Pension Roll,* in Vol. xiv, Sen. Doc. 514, 23rd Cong., 1st sess., 1833-34.

SIMPSON, JAMES, aged 79, resided in Randolph county, June 1, 1840, with William Simpson.—*Census of Pensioners,* 1841, p. 148.

SKANES, ADAM, aged 85, resided in Butler county, June 1, 1840, with Adam Skanes, sen.—*Census of Pensioners,* 1841 p. 149.

SLOAN, SAMUEL, aged 76, and a resident of Limestone county; private N. C. Continental Line; enrolled on February 29, 1832, under act of Congress of March 18, 1818, payment to date from February 24, 1832; annual allowance, $96; sums received to date of publication of list, $146.48.—*Revolutionary Pension Roll,* in Vol. xiv, Sen. Doc. 514, 23rd Cong., 1st sess., 1833-34.

SMITH, ISAAC. "The Rev. Isaac Smith, a native of Virginia, for three years an orderly sergeant in the army under Washington and Lafayette, the friend and host of Bishop Asbury, and other of the Bishops of the Church, for more than half a century a minister of the Gospel, serving the longest term at Asbury Mission of any man ever connected with it, and terminating his active ministry at that place, was a man of noble character, a model Christian, and he made an honorable record. 'Believing every word of God, meek above the reach of provocation, and thoroughly imbued with the spirit of love and devotion, he was a saint indeed.'

"An incident may be related here which will relate his patriotism, and which will indicate his fidelity to the ministry and his constant adherence to his religion. In August, 1824, Marquis De La Fayette, the friend of Washington and of American liberty, made a visit to the United States, landing at New York, and he was tendered a reception worthy of his patriotic services and worth yof the country whose liberty he had helped to achieve. The Senate and House of Representatives of the State of Alabama in General Assembly convened, at Cahawba, Alabama, passed, by unanimous vote, a resolution, which was approved December 24, 1824, as follows: 'And be it further resolved, That his excellency the Governor be requested to invite, in such manner as he shall deem most respectful, Major General La Fayette to honor the State of Alabama with a visit, and in the event of his acceptance of such invitation, he be received in such manner as shall best comport with the important services he has rendered the American people.' In pursuance of the resolution, Governor Pickens invited the distinguished guest of the nation to Alabama, and the invitation was accepted, and the visit was made. On March 31, 1825, the venerable and honored La Fayette under an escort of Georgians, halted, in the midst of the Creek National, upon the eastern bank of the Chattahoochee River, whose western side laves the soil of Alabama. The Georgia escort delivered the hero of American liberty, and their guest, to fifty nude and painted Creek Indian warriors. The Indians, vying with the citizens of the United States in the homage paid the noble Frenchman, conveyed him across the river and put him down on Alabama soil. He was then about one mile from the Asbury school. One of the first white men to greet La Fayette when he set foot on Alabama soil was the man who for three years attended him as orderly sergeant, and carried messages for him while the struggle for the independence of the American colonies went on. That man was the Rev. Isaac Smith, the Missionary in charge of the Asbury School for the Indians. They greeted, recollected, and recognized each other. There in the howling wilderness, and in the presence of painted warriors and naked savages, the old comrades in arms embraced each other, and gave expression to their friendship, and vent to their emotions, and the once young orderly, now a grave preacher of the Gospel and a devoted Missionary, prayed with and for the old Commander and patriot, and with deep emotion, strong faith, and earnest petitions commended him to the court of Heaven, and besought for him citizenship in the Kingdom of Christ, and the liberty which pertains to the sons of God. How anomalous and yet how appropriate all this! No event in all the course of that triumphal tour through the American continent made a deeper or more lasting impression upon the old patriot than that reunion of himself and the orderly sergeant of the former times, on the borders of Alabama. La Fayette tarried for the day, and he and Smith, the Missionary to the Indians, talked of the past and the present, in sweet counsel, and in the meantime witnessed one of those special contests and social pasttimes peculiar to the aborigines, a game of ball. The meeting of his old Commander at the very spot of his missionary labors was one of the unexpected pleasures which the Rev. Mr. Smith enjoyed beyond description. That meeting recollectetd the reminiscences of the past, revived his spirits, renewed his youth, strengthened his patriotism, and made an epoch in his eventful life.

"The Rev. Isaac Smith died in Monroe County, Georgia, at the age of seventy-six, and went to his eternal home. His children have honored him by religious lives."—Rev. Dr. Anson West's, *History of Methodism in Alabama,* pp. 380-2.

SMITH, JAMES, aged 81, resided in Jackson county, June 1, 1840, with James P. Smith.—*Census of Pensioners,* 1841, p. 148.

SMITH, JOHN, aged 69, and a resident of Madison county; private N. C. Militia; enrolled on September 26, 1833, under act of Congress of June 7, 1832, payment to date from March 4, 1831; annual allowance, $80.—*Revolutionary Pension Roll,* in Vol. xiv, Sen. Doc. 514, 23rd Cong., 1st sess., 1833-34. He resided in Jackson county, June 1, 1840, with Larkin Smith, aged 77.—*Census of Pensioners,* 1841, p. 148.

SMITH, JOHN, aged 73, and a resident of Bibb county; private S. C. Militia and Continental Line; enrolled on May 29, 1833, under act of Congress of June 7, 1832, payment to date from March 4, 1831; annual allowance, $80; sums received to date of publication of list, $240.—*Revolutionary Pension Roll,* in Part 3, Vol. xiii, Sen. Doc. 514, 23rd Cong., 1st sess., 1833-34.

SMITH, REBECCA, AGED 39, resided in Jackson county, June 1, 1840.—*Census of Pensioners,* 1841, p. 148.

SPLANN, CORNELIUS, age not given, a resident of Morgan county; sergeant 8th Regular U. S. Infantry; enrolled on October 15, 1818, payment to date from July 23, 1818; annual allowance, $48; sums received to date of publication of list, 557.69; Acts Military establishment.—*Revolutionary Pension Roll,* in Vol. xiv, Sen. Doc. 514, 2rd Cong., 1st sess., 1833-34.

STAFFORD, DAVID, aged 74, and a resident of Morgan county; private Virginia Continental Line; enrolled on May 16, 1826, under act of Congress of March 18, 1818, payment to date from April 22, 1826; annual allowance, $96; sums received to date of publication of list, $707.46.—*Revolutionary Pension Roll,* in Vol. xiv, Sen. Doc. 514, 23rd Cong., 1st sess., 1833-34.

STANFORD, THOMAS, age not given; resided in Marion county, June 1, 1840.—*Census of Pensioners,* 1841, p. 148.

STARNES, NICHOLAS, aged 78, and a resident of Jefferson county; private Virginia Militia; enrolled on July 18, 1834, under act of Congress of June 7, 1832, payment to date from March 4, 1831; annual allowance, $20.—*Revolutionary*

Revolutionary Soldiers in Alabama. 113

Pension Roll, in Vol. xiv, Sen .Doc. 514, 23rd Cong., 1st sess., 1833-34.

STEPHENS, REUBEN, aged 77, resided in Chambers county, June 1, 1840.—*Census of Pensioners*, 1841, p. 149.

STEWART, THOMAS, aged 76, and a resident of Autauga county; private N. C. State Troops; enrolled on August 12, 1833, under act of Congress of June 7, 1832, payment to date from March 4, 1831; annual allowance, $51.45; sums received to date of publication of list, $154.35.—*Revolutionary Pension Roll*, in Part 3, Vol. xiii, Sen. Doc. 514, 23rd Cong., 1st sess., 1833-34.

STONE, REUBEN, aged 79, and a resident of Madison county; private S. C. Continental Line; enrolled on January 4, 1834, under act of Congress of June 7, 1832, payment to date from March 4, 1831; annual allowance, $80.—*Revolutionary Pension Roll*, in Vol. xiv, Sen. Doc. 514, 23rd Cong., 1st sess., 1833-34.

STILLWAGON, ———. "Mrs. Elizabeth Stillwagon was accidentally burnt to death at Connellsville on the 6th. She was 115 years old, and her husband was a Revolutionary soldier."—*The Southern Advocate*, Huntsville, Feb. 22, 1854.

STOCKMON, CHRISTOPHER, a resident of Mobile county; private, particular service not shown; enrolled on May 20, 1834, under act of Congress of June 7, 1832, payment to date from March 4, 1831; annual allowance, $20; transferred from North Carolina.—*Pension Book*, State Branch Bank, Mobile.

STOKES, SYLVESTER, aged 35, and a resident of Lawrence county; private Virginia Continental Line; enrolled on March 14, 1827, under act of Congress of March 18, 1818, payment to date from February 2, 1827; annual allowance, $96; sums received to date of publication of list, $536.51.— *Revolutionary Pension Roll*, in Vol. xiv, Sen. Doc. 514, 23rd Cong., 1st sess., 1833-34.

STORY, HENRY, aged 77, and a resident of Greene county; sergeant S. C. Militia; enrolled on July 2, 1833, under act of Congress of June 7, 1832; payment to date from March 4, 1831; annual allowance, $120; sums received to date of publication of list, $360.—*Revoultionary Pension Roll*, in Vol. xiv, Sen. Doc. 514, 23rd Cong., 1st sess., 1833-34.

STRANGE, ABNER A., aged 73, and a resident of Limestone county; private and sergeant Virginia Continental Militia; enrolled on February 23, 1833, under act of Congress of June 7, 1832; payment to date from March 4, 1831; annual allowance, 40; sums received to date of publication of list, $100.—*Revolutionary Pension Roll,* in Vol. xiv, Sen. Doc. 514, 23rd Cong., 1st sess., 1833-34.

STRONG, JOHNSON, aged 75, and a resident of Fayette county; private Virginia Militia; enrolled on January 9, 1834, under act of Congress of June 7, 1832, payment to date from March 4, 1831; annual allowance, $33; sums received to date of publication of list, $99.—*Revolutionary Pension Roll,* in Vol. xiv, Sen. Doc. 514, 23rd Cong., 1st sess., 1833-34. He resided in Fayette county, June 1, 1840, aged 82.—*Census of Pensioners,* 1841, p. 148.

STROUEL, MATHEW, aged 87, and a resident of Shelby county; private N. C. State Troops; enrolled on June 17, 1834, under act of Congress of June 7, 1832, payment to date from March 4, 1831; annual allowance, $20.—*Rveloutionary Pension Roll,* in Vol. xiv, Sen. Doc. 514, 23rd Cong., 1st sess., 1833-34. Also resided in Bibb county.—*Pension Book,* State Branch Bank, Mobile.

STUDROE, READY, enrolled under act of Congress of March 18, 1818; no further details given.—*Pension Book,* State Branch Bank, Mobile.

STURDEVANT, JOHN. "At his residence, in Summerfield, Dallas county, of apoplexy, on Saturday morning, the 21st December, 1856, ROBERT STURDEVANT, ESQ., one of the oldest citizens of this county.

"Mr. Sturdevant was born in Dinwiddie county, Virginia, on the 28th July, 1789, and was the son of Mr. John Sturdevant, a soldier of the Revolution. Mr. S. was brought to Hancock, Georgia, when quite young, by his father, and remained there until 1818, when he removed to Alabama.

"We knew Mr. Sturdivant, by report and personally, for the greater portion of our life, and when we came to Selma to reside, in 1845, he gave us the warmest and heartiest welcome. He was kind, liberal and hospitable—a sincere christian—a charitable man—a good friend of ours, and it is with profound sorrow we record his death."—*The Dallas Gazete,* Jan. 9, 1857.

SUTTON, GEORGE, age not given, a resident of Mobile county; private 7th Reg. U. S. Infantry; enrolled on April 18, 1825, payment to date from January 28, 1825; annual al-

Revolutionary Soldiers in Alabama. 115

lowance, $96; sums received to date of publication of list, $826.10; Acts Military establishment.—*Revolutionary Pension Roll,* in Vol. xiv, Sen. Doc. 514, 23rd Cong., 1st sess., 1833-34.

SUTTON, ROBERT, aged 76, and a resident of Lawrence county; private S. C. Continental Line; enrolled on January 24 ,1824, under act of Congress of March 18, 1818, payment to date from November 10, 1823; annual allowance, $96; sums received to date of publication of list, $950.66.—*Revolutionary Pension Roll,* in Vol. xiv, Sen. Doc. 514, 23rd Cong., 1st sess., 1833-34.

TABOR, WILLIAM, aged 73, and a resident of Bibb county; ensign and lieutenant N. C. Militia; enrolled on January 2, 1834, under act of Congress of June 7, 1832, payment to date from March 4, 1831; annual allowance, $100; sums received to date of publication of list, $300.—*Revolutionary Pension Roll,* in Part 3, Vol. xiii, Sen. Doc. 514, 23rd Cong., 1st sess., 1833-34.

TALIAFERRO, RICHARD. Mildred, wife of Richard Taliaferro, who was a resident of Pickens county, captain of infantry; enrolled on August 4, 1838, under act of Congress of June 7, 1832, payment to date from March 4, 1831; annual allowance, $480.—*Pension Book,* State Branch Bank, Mobile. Mildred Taliaferro resided in Pickens county, June 1, 1840, aged 78.—*Census of Pensioners,* 1841, p. 148.

TARRANT, JAMES, sen., aged 86, resided in Jefferson county, June 1, 1840, with James Tarrant, Jr.—*Census of Pensioners,* 1841, p. 149.

TATOM, THOMAS. "Mr. Clay, yielding to his feelings excited in behalf of the son of a Revolutionary Patriot, who was captured at Mier, a citizen of Alabama, addressed a letter to President Santa Anna, requesting his liberation. We understand that he has just received a polite letter from Santa Anna, informing him of the prompt discharge of the captive according to his request."—*Lexington Observer.*

[The person alluded to above was Mr. Thomas Tatom, son of Capt. Tatom of Morgan county, Ala.]—*Ed. Adv. Southern Advocate,* Huntsville, Oct. 25, 1844, p. 2.

A TOUCHING INCSDENT.

"While Capt. Nicholas Davis was making a tour through the county of Lauderdale filling some political appointments, and while at Rogersville awaiting the assembling of the people whom he was to address, the western mail-stage came in, and in a few moments, a strange young man rushing into the room where Capt. Davis was, and almost without salutation, throwing his arms around Capt. Davis' neck and submerged in tears, hailed him as his deliverer. The company astonished, withdrew for a moment, supposing the young man to be some near relative. Capt. Davis also wept when he was embracing *Thomas Tatom,* one of the Texas prisoners, who was released by the friendly interposition of himself through Mr. Clay of Kentucky. The whole company partook of the general joy. The young man was on his way home, to his father's house at least, where he would meet the full-heart, and the affectionate embraces of a time-worn father, and a large circle of relatives and friends."—*Athens Whig.*—*Southern Advocate,* Huntsville, Oct. 25, 1844, p. 3.

TAYLOR, ELIJAH, aged 81, and a resident of Limestone county; private and sergeant N. C. Militia; enrolled on July 29, 1834, under act of Congress of June 7, 1832, payment to date from March 4, 1831; annual allowance, $33.33.—*Revolutionary Pension Roll,* in Vol. xiv, Sen. Doc. 514, 23rd Cong., 1st sess., 1833-34.

TAYLOR, GEORGE. "This Revolutionary soldier is mentioned in *Northern Alabama Illustrated,* p. 261. He is buried ten miles east of Huntsville, near the bank of the Flint river; there is no tombstone over his grave. Family records give the facts of his history. George Taylor was born in Virginia, exact date not known but about 1762, and died in Madison county, Alabama, 1826. He entered the Revolutionary army in his seventeenth year, was first under fire at the battle of Monmouth, 1778, then came to South Carolina with 'Light Horse Harry' Lee's command and engaged in many battles and skirmishes with Lee, and at the close of the war he was a lieutenant. 'He was in the disasterous charge at King's Bridge, where, owing to misdirection of orders, the advance was not supported and out of twenty, only five made good their retreat.' Soon after the Revolution he married Miss Jennings, of Lexington, Oglethorpe county, Georgia, and she was probably born in Lexington. Miles Jennings, a famous Indian fighter, who is described in White's *Historical Collections of Georgia,* and who lived in Oglethorpe county, is perhaps of the same family as the wife of George Taylor. It is stated that George Taylor commanded a scouting party for defense against the Indians, for more than ten years after the close of the Revolutionary war; this party being organized at Lexington, Georgia. He was also captain in the militia. He

Revolutionary Soldiers in Alabama.   117

moved from Georgia to Winchester, Tenn., in 1805, and came to Madison county, Ala., in 1810, and settled on the banks of the Flint river, where he is buried. His wife died in Alabama several years before his death. He died in 1826. A grandson of this couple was the late Judge Thomas J. Taylor, of Huntsville, probate judge of Madison county. The inherited courageous and patriotic spirit of the family is shown by the fact that Judge Taylor and six brothers were gallant soldiers and officers in the Confederate States army. A great-grandson, Douglass Taylor, is now living in Huntsville, and other descendents are living in Louisiana."—Mrs. P. H. Mell in *Transactions* of the Alabama Historical Society, Vol. iv, pp. 566-567.

TAYLOR, MEREDITH, a resident of Pickens county; private, particular service not shown; enrolled on November 11, 1837, under act of Congress of June 7, 1832; annual allowance, $46.66; transferred from South Carolina.—*Pension Book,* State Branch Bank, Mobile. He resided in Pickens county, June 1, 1840, with James Bonner, aged 78.—*Census of Pensioners,* 1841, p. 149.

TAYLOR, THOMAS, aged 56, resided in Chambers county, June 1, 1840, with Jonathan Music.—*Census of Pensioners,* 1841, p. 149.

TEMPLE, JOHN, aged 76, and a resident of Montgomery county; private Virginia Continental Line; enrolled on December 14, 1819, under act of Congress of March 18, 1818; payment to date from July 23, 1818; annual allowance, $96; sums received to date of publication of list, $1,451.38; transferred from Edgefield district, S. C., from March 4, 1830.—*Revolutionary Pension Roll,* in Vol. xiv, Sen. Doc. 514, 23rd Cong., 1st sess., 1833-34.

THIGPEN, JOSEPH, aged 76, and a resident of Perry county; private N. C. Militia; enrolled on September 24, 1833, under act of Congress of June 7, 1832, payment to date from March 4, 1831; annual allowance, $20; sums received to date of publication of list, $50.—*Revolutionary Pension Roll,* in Vol. xiv, Sen. Doc. 514, 23rd Cong., 1st sess., 1833-34.

THOMAS, JOHN, sen., aged 81, resided in Autauga county, June 1, 1840, with Mary Johnson.—*Census of Pensioners,* 1841, p. 149.

THOMPSON, BENJAMIN, aged 72, and a resident of Montgomery county; private S. C. Militia; enrolled on January 4, 1834, under act of Congress of June 7, 1832, payment to date from March 4, 1831; annual allowance, $80; sums received to date of publication of list, $200.—*Revolutionary Pension Roll,* in Vol. xiv, Sen. Doc. 514, 23rd Cong., 1st sess., 1833-34.

THOMPSON, ELECTROUS, aged 78, and a resident of Morgan county; private Maryland Continental Line; enrolled on September 17, 1833, under act of Congress of June 7, 1832, payment to date from March 4, 1831; annual allownace, $50; sums received to date of publication of list, $125.—*Revolutionary Pension Roll,* in Vol. xiv, Sen. Doc. 514, 23rd Cong., 1st sess., 1833-34. He resided in Morgan county, June 1, 1840, aged 91.—*Census of Pensioners,* 1841, p. 148.

THOMPSON, NICHOLAS, aged 75, and a resident of Morgan county; private N. C. Continental Line; enrolled on April 3, 1824, under act of Congress of March 18, 1818, payment to date from January 12, 1824; annual allowance, $96; sums received to date of publication of list, $962.22.—*Revolutionary Pension Roll,* in Vol. xiv, Sen. Doc. 514, 23rd Cong., 1st sess., 1833-34. He resided in Morgan county, June 1, 1840, aged 81.—*Census of Pensioners,* 1841, p. 148.

THOMPSON, ROBERT, aged 74, and a resident of Franklin county; private Virginia Continental Line; enrolled on April 21, 1824, under act of Congress of March 18, 1818, payment to date from February 2, 1824; annual allowance, $96; sums received to date of publication of list, $632.53.—*Revolutionary Pension Roll,* in Vol. xiv, Sen. Doc. 514, 23rd Cong., 1st sess., 1833-34.

TIDMORE, JOHN, aged 84, resided in Greene county, June 1, 1840.—*Census of Pensioners,* 1841, p. 149.

TINEY, ROBERT, aged 81, and a resident of Lawrence county; private S. C. Continental Line; enrolled on April 26, 1828, under act of Congress of March 18, 1818, payment to date from February 6, 1828; annual allowance, $96; sums received to date of publication of list, $439.—*Revolutionary Pension Roll,* in Vol. xiv, Sen. Doc. 514, 23rd Cong., 1st sess., 1833-34.

TOLBERT,SAMUEL, aged 87, resided in Benton county, June 1, 1840.—*Census of Pensioners,* 1841, p. 148.

TOWNSEL, JOSHUA, aged 80, resided in Jackson county, June 1, 1840.—*Census of Pensioners,* 1841, p. 148.

Revolutionary Soldiers in Alabama. 119

TOWNSEND, ANDREW, aged 71, and a resident of St. Clair county; private S. C. Militia; enrolled on September 28, 1833, under act of Congress of June 7, 1832; payment to date from March 4, 1831; annual allowance, $20; sums received to date of publication of list, $50.—*Revolutionary Pension Roll,* in Vol. xiv, Sen .Doc. 514, 23rd Cong., 1st sess., 1833-34.

TRENCH, BENJAMIN, aged 69, and a resident of Limestone county; private Virginia Continental Line; enrolled on June 6, 1820, under act of Congress of March 18, 1818, payment to date from October 17, 1818; annual allowance, $96; sums received to date of publication of list, $486.99. Dropped under act May 1, 1820. Restored, commencing January 5, 1830.—*Revolutionary Pension Roll,* in Vol. xiv, Sen. Doc. 514, 23rd Cong., 1st sess., 1833-34.

TRIBBLE, ELIJAH, aged 80, and a resident of Jackson county; private N. C. Militia; enrolled on January 4, 1834, under act of Congress of June 7, 1832, payment to date from March 4, 1831; annual allowance, $20; sums received to date of publication of list, $60.—*Revolutionary Pension Roll,* in Vol. xiv, Sen. Doc. 514, 23rd Cong., 1st sess., 1833-34.

TRIBBLE, JAMES, aged 78, and a resident of Madison county; private Virginia Militia; enrolled on January 24, 1833, under act of Congress of June 7, 1832, payment to date from March 4, 1831; annual allowance, $40; sums received to date of publication of list, $100.—*Revolutionary Pension Roll,* in Vol. xiv, Sen. Doc. 514, 23rd Cong., 1st sess., 1833-34.

TRUITT, WILLIAMS. Williams Truitt lies buried at Teller's ferry on Lynch's creek. His daughter married William Chancellor, son of Jerry Chancellor. The Chancellors of Coosa county are descendants. These facts were furnished by D. B. Oden, Childersburg, Ala. See *Transactions* of the Alabama Historical Society, Vol. iv, p. 567.

TUBBS, JOHN, SR., aged 76, and a resident of Perry county; private S. C. State Troops; enrolled on June 17, 1834, under act of June 7, 1832, payment to date from March 4, 1831; annual allowance, $26.21.—*Revolutionary Pension Roll,* in Vol. xiv, Sen. Doc. 514, 23rd Cong., 1st sess., 1833-34.

TUCKER, GEORGE, aged 89, and a resident of Fayette county; private N .C. Continental Line; enrolled on February 10, 1834, under act of Congress of June 7, 1832; payment to date from March 4, 1831; annual allowance, $46.66; sums received to date of publication of list, $139.98.—*Revolutionary*

Pension Roll, in Vol. xiv, Sen. Doc. 514, 23rd Cong., 1st sess., 1833-34. Also resided in Marion county.—*Pension Book,* State Branch Bank, Mobile. He also resided in Marion county.—*Pension Book,* State Branch Bank, Mobile.

TURNER, LEWIS, aged 72, and a resident of Shelby county; private S. C. Militia; enrolled on January 4, 1834, under act of Congress of June 7, 1832, payment to date from March 4, 1831; annual allowance, $40.—*Revolutionary Pension Roll,* in Vol. xiv, Sen. Doc. 514, 23rd Cong., 1st sess., 1833-34.

TURNER, NOEL, a resident of Mobile county; private, particular service not shown; enrolled on March 21, 1836, under act of Congress of June 7, 1832, payment to date from March 4, 1831; annual allowance, $20; died January 21, 1837. —*Pension Book,* State Branch Bank, Mobile.

UPTON, GEORGE, a resident of DeKalb county; private, particular service not shown; enrolled on July 31, 1833, under act of Congress of June 7, 1832; annual allowance, $30.—*Pension Book,* State Branch Bank, Mobile. He resided in DeKalb county, June 1, 1840, aged 80.—*Census of Pensioners,* 1841, p. 148.

VARNER, JOSEPH, a resident of Clarke county; private, particular service not shown; enrolled on May 8, 1832, under act of Congress of June 7, 1832, payment to date from September 4, 1835; annual allowance, $72.—*Pension Book,* State Branch Bank, Mobile.

VAUGHAN, INGRAHAM, aged 77, and a resident of Lauderdale county, private captain and sergeant Virginia Continental Line and Militia; enrolled on May 14, 1834, under act of Congress of June 7, 1832, payment to date from March 4, 1831; annual allowance, $57.11.—*Revolutionary Pension Roll,* in Vol. xiv, Sen. Doc. 514, 23rd Cong., 1st sess., 1833-34.

VAUGHAN, JOEL, aged 95, and a resident of Pickens county; private N. C. Continental Line; enrolled on February 27, 1834, under act of Congress of June 7, 1832, payment to date from March 4, 1831; annual allowance, $48.32; sums received to date of publication of list, $144.96.—*Revolutionary Pension Roll,* in Vol. xiv, Sen. Doc. 514, 23rd Cong., 1st sess., 1833-34.

WAGSTER, WILLIAM, age not given, and a resident of Butler county; private S. C. Continental Line; enrolled on

July 16, 1819, under act of Congress of March 18, 1818; payment to date from July 5, 1819; annual allowance, $96; suspended under act May 1, 1820. Continued and transferred from Edgefield District, S. C., from January 22, 1829.—*Revolutionary Pension Roll,* in Vol. xiv, Sen. Doc. 514, 23rd Cong., 1st sess., 1833-34.

WAID (sic), CALVIN, aged 73, and a resident of Blount county; private New Jersey Militia; enrolled on July 10, 1834, under act of Congress of June 7, 1832, payment to date from March 4, 1831; annual allowance, $53.33.—*Revolutionary Pension Roll,* in Part 3, Vol .xiii, Sen. Doc. 514, 23rd Cong., 1st sess., 1833-34.

WALDEN, DAVID, aged 76, and a resident of Blount county; private N. C. Continental Line; enrolled on January 27, 1834, under act of Congress of June 7, 1832, payment to date from March 4, 1831; annual allowance, $80.—*Revolutionary Pension Roll,* in Part 3, Vol. xiii, Sen. Doc. 514, 23rd Cong,. 1st sess., 1833-34.

WALDRON, CHARLES, aged 75, and a resident of Lowndes county; private Maryland Militia; enrolled on May 19, 1834, under act of Congress of June 7, 1832, payment to date from March 4, 1831; annual allowance, $20.—*Revolutionary Pension Roll,* in Vol. xiv, Sen. Doc. 514, 23rd Cong., 1st sess., 1833-34.

WALKER, TANDY, private, particular service not shown; enrolled on September 20, 1838, payment to date from January 1, 1828; annual allowance, $96.—*Pension Book,* State Branch Bank, Mobile.

WALKER, WILLIAM, aged 78, resided in DeKalb county, June 1, 1840, with G. Walker.—*Census of Pensioners,* 1841, p. 148.

WALLACE, JOHN, aged 75, and a resident of Bibb county; private N. C. Militia; enrolled on June 17, 1834, under act of Congress of June 7, 1832, payment to date from March 4, 1831; annual allowance, $80.—*Revolutionary Pension Roll,* in Part 3, Vol. xiii, Sen. Doc. 514, 23rd Cong., 1st sess., 1833-34. He resided in Bibb county, June 1, 1840, aged 80 to 90.—*Census of Pensioners,* 1841, p. 149.

WALLING, DAVID, aged 76, resided in Walker county, June 1, 1840.—*Census of Pensioners,* 1841, p. 150.

WALLING, WILLIAM, aged 73, and a resident of Madison county; private and sergeant S. C. Militia; enrolled on

November 4, 1833, under act of Congress of June 7, 1832, payment to date from March 4, 1831; annual allowance, $35; sums received to date or publication of list, $105.—*Revolutionary Pension Roll,* in Vol. xiv, Sen. Doc. 514, 23rd Cong., 1st sess., 1833-34.

WALTON, WILLIAM, aged 68, and a resident of Greene county; private N. C. Militia; enrolled on January 16, 1833, under act of Congress of June 7, 1832, payment to date from March 4, 1831; annual allowance, $33.33; sums received to date of publication of list, $99.99.—*Revolutionary Pension Roll,* in Vol. xiv, Sen. Doc. 514, 23rd Cong., 1st sess., 1833-34.

WARD, CALVIN, private, particular service not shown; annual allowance, $53.33; records do not show that any payment was ever made.—*Pension Book,* State Branch Bank, Mobile.

WARD, JOHN, aged 77, and a resident of Bibb county; private N. C. Militia; enrolled January 4, 1834, under act of Congress of June 7, 1832, payment to date from March 4, 1831; annual allowance, $30.—*Revolutionary Pension Roll,* in Part 3, Vol. xiii, Sen. Doc. 514, 23rd Cong., 1st sess., 1833-34.

WARDEN, SAMUEL, aged 84, resided in Benton county, June 1, 1840, with David Barnwell.—*Census of Pensioners,* 1841, p. 148.

WARSHAM, JOHN, aged 72, and a resident of Washington county; private Virginia Continental Line; enrolled on February 10, 1834, under act of Congress of June 7, 1832, payment to date from March 4, 1831; annual allowance, $30; sums received to date of publication of list, $90.—*Revolutionary Pension Roll,* in Vol. xiv, Sen. Doc. 514, 23rd Cong., 1st sess., 1833-34. He resided in Washington county, June 1, 1840, aged 78.—*Census of Pensioners,* 1841, p. 150.

WATFORD, JOSEPH, aged 92, resided in Dale county, June 1, 1840, with Barnabas Whatford.—*Census of Pensioners,* 1841, p. 149.

WATKINS, JAMES, aged 92, resided in Benton county, June 1, 1840.—*Census of Pensioners,* 1841, p. 148.

WATTS, GARRETT, aged 78, and a resident of Perry county; private N. C. Militia; enrolled on July 16, 1834, under act of Congress of June 7, 1832, payment to date from March 4, 1831; annual allowance, $23.33.—*Revolutionary Pen-*

sion Roll, in Vol. xiv, Sen. Doc. 514, 23rd Cong., 1st sess., 1833-34.

WEBSTER, JOHN, "John Webster was born in Caroline county, Va., in 1743. Early in the struggle for independence he enlisted in the Continental army and served under General Washington. He was with the American army at Yorktown, and witnessed the surrender of Cornwallis. In 1817 he came to Alabama and during the last ten years of his life he lived in Tuscaloosa with his son, John J. Webster. He died in Tuscaloosa, September 6, 1839, in the 97th year of his age.—See Tuscaloosa *Flag of the Union, September* 14, 1839.

"It is shown by the records in Washington, D. C., that one John Webster served as a private in Captain Alexander S. Dandridge's troop, 1st regiment of Light Dragoons, commanded by Colonel Bland, Continental troops, Revolutionary War. He was 'appointed' July 20, 1777, to serve until December 1, 1778, and his name last appears on a pay roll for the month of November, 1778. It is also shown by the records that one John Webster served as a private in Captain Thomas Pry's company in a regiment of foot commanded by Colonel Moses Hazen, Continental troops, Revolutionary War. He enlisted April 16, 1777, to serve during the war; joined the company June 17, 1777, and his name last appears on an account covering the period from June 1 to July 31, 1779.

"It is further shown by the records that one John Webster served as a carpenter in Captain Low's company, Corps of Artificers, Continental troops, Revolutionary War. He enlisted April 3, 1777, to serve to January 1, 1778, and his name last appears as that of a clerk on the roll for the period from August 3, to November 27, 1778, with remark 'appointed September 1, 1778.'

"It is hardly probable that these are one and the same individual."—Mrs. P. H. Mell in *Transactions* of the Alabama Historical Society, Vol. iv, p. 568.

WELBORN, ISAAC, aged 76, and a resident of Madison county; private N. C. Continental Line and Militia; enrolled on January 24, 1833, under act of Congress of June 7, 1833, payment to date from March 4, 1831; annual allowance, $53.33.—*Revolutionary Pension Roll,* in Vol. xiv, Sen. Doc. 514, 23rd Cong., 1st sess., 1833-34.

WEST, SAMUEL, aged 103, resided in Marshall county, June 1, 1840, with Butcher West.—*Census of Pensioners,* 1841, p. 148.

WESTON, ROBERT. "Robert Weston, a soldier from North Carolina, is buried at 'Shady Grove,' Sumter county, Ala. His tomb records simply his birth and death and 'A Revolutionary Soldier.' A few brief facts of his history have been furnished by Mrs. M. C. Carpenter, his granddaughter, of Eutaw, Ala. Robert Weston was born in England, August 29, 1763, and died in Sumter county, Alabama, July 21, 1845, aged 81 years, 5 months and 8 days.

"He came to America when a mere lad, with his two brothers, Isaac and Frank Weston. Although very young, he fought in the Revolution in North Carolina; was brave and quickwitted; was captured three times and sentenced to death, but made his escape each time through shrewd ability in disguising himself. He married Mary Ogilvie of South Carolina, who was born June 26, 1769, and died January 11, 1845, aged 75 years, 5 months and 15 days. The young couple settled in Fairfield district, S. C., where they resided until their children were grown. They had a large family and many descendants are still living in South Carolina, Alabama, Mississippi and Texas. One son, I. M. Weston, settled in Columbia, S. C., but the other children all removed to Alabama. Naturally the old couple followed their children and came to Sumter county, Ala., in 1833, where they purchased a home near their children and spent their old age in peace and contentment surrounded by children and grandchildren. Robert Weston was a man of intelligence and excellent education and his grandchildren remember him with the deepest affection and respect. His thrilling stories of Revolutionary times are yet remembered and told in the family."—Mrs. P. H. Mell in *Transactions* of the Alabama Historical Society, Vol. iv, pp. 568-569.

WHITE, ANDREW, aged 72, and a resident of Lawrence county; private N. C. Militia; enrolled on April 23, 1833, under act of Congress of June 7, 1832, payment to date from March 4, 1831; annual allowance, $20.—*Revolutionary Pension Roll*, in Vol. xiv, Sen .Doc. 514, 23rd Cong., 1st sess., 1833-34. He resided in Lawrence county, June 1, 1840, aged 78.—*Census of Pensioners*, 1841, p. 148.

WHITE, ELIJAH, aged 78, resided in Franklin county, June 1, 1840, with Samuel B. White.—*Census of Pensioners*, 1841, p. 148.

WHITE, JAMES, aged 73, and a resident of Jackson county; private Virginia Continental Line; enrolled on January 2, 1834, under act of Congress of June 7, 1832, payment

Revolutionary Soldiers in Alabama.   125

to date from March 4, 1831; annual allowance, $40; sums received to date of publication of list, $120.—*Revolutionary Pension Roll,* in Vol. xiv, Sen. Doc. 514, 23rd Cong., 1st sess., 1833-34.

WHITEFIELD, WILLIAM, aged 84, and a resident of St. Clair county; private Virginia Continental Line; enrolled on January 18, 1830, under act of Congress of March 18, 1818, payment to date from January 18, 1830; annual allowance, $96; sums received to date of publication of list, $396.64. —*Revolutionary Pension Roll,* in Vol. xiv, Sen. Doc. 514, 23rd Cong., 1st sess., 1833-34.

WICKER, WILLIAM. "Died in Pike county, Ala., on Sunday, the 20th December last, Mr. William Wicker. The deceased was aged 106 years. He served as a soldier in the Revolutionary war. He was in the battle of Eutaw Springs, and was engaged in several skirmishes with the British and Tories under General Marion of South Carolina."—*Spirit of the South.*—*The Southern Advocate,* Huntsville, March 9, 1853. As a private, particular service not being shown, he was enrolled for pension under act of Congress of June 7, 1832, payment to date from March 4, 1831; annual allowance, $20; records do not show that any payment was ever made.— *Pension Book,* State Branch Bank, Mobile.

WIGINGTON, GEORGE, aged 72, and a resident of Pickens county; private N. C. State troops; enrolled on January 9, 1834. under act of Congress of June 7, 1832, payment to date from March 4, 1831; annual allowance, $30; sums received to date of publication of list, $90.—*Revolutionary Pension Roll,* in Vol. xiv, Sen. Doc. 514, 23rd Cong., 1st sess., 1833-34.

WILDER, GEORGE, aged 73, and a resident of Shelby county; private Virginia Militia; enrolled on March 5, 1833, under act of Congress of June 7, 1832, payment to date from March 4, 1831; annual allowance, $20.—*Revolutionary Pension Roll,* in Vol. xiv, Sen. Doc. 514, 23rd Cong., 1st sess., 1833-34. Resided also in Talladega county.—*Pension Book,* State Branch Bank, Mobile.

WILKINSON, JOHN, aged 82, and a resident of Wilcox county; private Virginia Militia; enrolled on September 28, 1834, under act of Congress of June 7, 1832, payment to date from March 4, 1831; annual allowance, $80; sums received to date of publication of list, $200.—*Revolutionary Pension Roll,* in Vol. xiv, Sen. Doc. 514, 23rd Cong., 1st sess., 1833-34.

WILLIAM, ISAAC; age not given, a resident of Greene county; captain in Cannon's regiment; enrolled on April 20, 1818, payment to date from December 26, 1813; annual allowance, $120; sums received, $800.19; and "on account of increased ratio of disability," rate increased to annual allowance of $180, under which $2,137.89 received to date of publication of list.—*Revolutionary Pension Roll,* in Vol. xiv, Sen. Doc. 514, 23rd Cong., 1st sess., 1833-34.

WILLIAMS, JOHN, aged 77, and a resident of Mobile county; private Virginia State Troops; enrolled on Nov. 22, 1833, under act of Congress of June 7, 1832, payment to date from March 4, 1831; annual allowance, $80; sums received to date of publication of list, $240.—*Revolutionary Pension Roll,* in Vol. xiv, Sen .Doc. 514, 23rd Cong., 1st sess., 1833-34. He resided in Mobile county, June 1, 1840, aged 86.—*Census of Pensioners,* 1841, p. 149. In the Census List, however, he is given a middle name, the entry being John Bailey Williams.

WILLIAMS, PETER, aged 78, and a resident of Pickens county; private S. C. Militia; enrolled on January 17, 1834, under act of Congress of June 7, 1832, payment to date from March 4, 1831; annual allowance, $50; sums received to date of publication of list, $150.—*Revolutionary Pension Roll,* in Vol. xiv, Sen. Doc. 514, 23rd Cong., 1st sess., 1833-34. He resided in Pickens county, June 1, 1840, aged 86.—*Census of Pensioners,* 1841, p. 149.

WILLIAMS, SAMUEL, a resident of Covington county; private, particular service not shown; enrolled on January 15, 1836, under act of Congress of June 7, 1832, payment to date from March 4, 1831, annual allowance, $80.—*Pension Book,* State Branch Bank, Mobile. He resided in Covington county, June 1, 1840, aged 86.—*Census of Pensioners,* 1841, p. 149.

WILLIAMSON, HAWLEY. "Died—On the 18th inst. [May], at his residence in this county, in the 78th year of his age, Hawley Williamson, a soldier of the Revolution, and for many years a citizen of Alabama."—*The Democrat,* Huntsville, May 28, 1830.

WILSON, JOHN, aged 74, and a resident of Bibb county; private Virginia Militia; enrolled on April 15, 1833, under act of Congress of June 7, 1832, payment to date from March 4, 1831; annual allowance, $43.33; sums received to date of publication of list, $129.99.—*Revolutionary Pension Roll,* in Part 3, Vol. xiii, Sen. Doc. 514, 23rd Cong., 1st sess., 1833-34. A resident of Bibb county.

Revolutionary Soldiers in Alabama. 127

WILSON, JOSHUA, aged 74, and a resident of Dallas county; private N. C. Continental Line; enrolled on March 1, 1834, under act of Congress of June 7, 1832, payment to date from March 4, 1831; annual allowance, $78.33; sums received to date of publication of list, $234.99.—*Revolutionary Pension Roll,* in Vol. xiv, Sen. Doc. 514, 23rd Cong., 1st sess., 1833-34. He resided in Clarke county, June 1, 1840, aged 80.—*Census of Pensioners,* 1841, p. 149. Also resided in Clarke county.—*Pension Book,* State Branch Bank, Mobile.

WILSON, ROBERT, aged 76, and a resident of Morgan county; private N. C. Continental Line; enrolled on February 1, 1827, under act of Congress of March 18, 1818, payment to date from December 6, 1826; annual allowance, $96; sums received to date of publication of list, $657.73.—*Revolutionary Pension Roll,* in Vol. xiv, Sen. Doc. 514, 23rd Cong., 1st sess., 1833-34.

WINN, ELISHA, age not given, a resident of Madison county; private Virginia Continental Line; enrolled on July 21, 1819, under act of Congress of March 18, 1818, payment to date from April 30, 1818; annual allowance, $96; died.—*Revolutionary Pension Roll,* in Vol. xiv, Sen. Doc. 514, 23rd Cong., 1st sess., 1833-34.

WINN, GALANUS, aged 74, and a resident of Madison county; private Virginia Militia; enrolled on December 18, 1833, under act of Congress of June 7, 1832, payment to date from March 4, 1831; annual allowance, $43.89; sums received to date of publication of list, $131.67.—*Revolutionary Pension Roll,* in Vol. xiv, Sen. Doc. 514, 23rd Cong., 1st sess. ,1833-34.

WINSTON, ANTHONY. "Captain Anthony Winston, of Hanover county, Virginia, a member of the Virginia convention of 1775, and a gallant captain in the Revolutionary army, lies buried in the old Winston family burying ground just out of Sheffield, Alabama. Vol. xiii, Daughters of the American Revolution *Lineage Book,* states that Anthony Winston was born in Hanover county, Virginia, in 1750, married Keziah Jones and died in Alabama in 1828. He was a delegate from Buckingham county to the convention of 1775; he afterwards served in the militia and rose to the rank of captain. Brewer's *Alabama* says that 'he was a colonial officer of 1776 and the owner of the celebrated Portuguese giant, Peter Francisco. Capt. Winston removed first to Tennessee and subsequently settled in Madison county, Alabama, about the year 1810. He was a man of marked and elevated character.' He died in

1828. He left seven sons, Anthony, John J., William, Joel W., Isaac, Edmund and Thomas J., and two daughters, Mrs. John Pettus (Alice T.) and Mrs. Jesse Jones. Capt. Winston was nearly related to Patrick Henry (a first cousin) and distinction is hereditary in the Winston family. He has many honored descendants; one of his grandsons was Governor John Anthony Winston of Sumter, the 'first native born governor of Alabama.' Another grandson is General Edmund Winston Pettus, now senator in the United States Congress. Another distinguished grandson was the brother of Gen. Pettus, Governor John J. Pettus, the war governor of Mississippi. Other descendants of Capt. Anthony Winston are scattered all over the Southwest, filling honorable positions with credit.

"The ancestry of Capt. Winston is thus given: Slaughter's *St. Mark's Parish* states that Isaac Winston, the most remote ancestor, was born in Yorkshire, England, in 1620. A grandson of his pursued his fortunes in Wales, where he had a large family. Three of his sons emigrated to America, and settled near Richmond, Va., in 1704. Their names were William, Isaac and James. Anthony Winston was descended from Isaac.

"(1) Isaac Winston, the emigrant, married Mary Dabney and died in Hanover county in 1760, leaving six children, William, Isaac, Anthony, Lucy, Mary Ann and Sarah. Sarah was the mother of Patrick Henry.

"(2) Anthony Winston (son of Isaac) married Alice, daughter of Col. James Taylor of Caroline; issue: Sarah, died single; Capt. Anthony Winston; Alice, married Judge Edmund Winston; Mary.

"We are indebted to Gen. Edmund Pettus, of the United States Senate, for the following facts, and a copy of the scription upon the tombstone:

Sacred to the memory
of
Anthony Winston and Keziah his wife,
He
Was born on the 15th of Nov. 1750
She
On the 10th of Feb. 1760.
They
Were married on the 11th day of Mar. 1776
She
Died October 1826 and he in 1828
——(*)

This tribute of respect
Is
Paid to the memory of the best of parents
By
Their grateful
and
Affectionate sons.

"They were buried at the family burying-ground on the plantation of their son, Anthony Winston, about one mile from Tuscumbia, in Colbert county, in the direction of Sheffield. Anthony Winston, here mentioned on this tombstone, was the son of Anthony Winston of Hanover county, Virginia, who was born September 29th, 1723, and married February 29th, 1747, Alice Taylor, daughter of James Taylor and Alice Thornton. He was born in Hanover county, but moved in his young days to Buckingham county, Virginia. He was a captain in the Revolutionary War. He was married in 1776, and went into the army a few months afterwards.

"The family has now in their possession a counterpane made of cotton which Mrs. Keziah Winston raised. She picked the cotton, spun the thread and wove the cloth, and then ornamented it by needle work like a Marseilles counterpane, whilst her husband was in the army. This old heirloom is perfectly preserved, and looks as well as it ever did but, of course, it is not used.

"Anthony Winston told his grandchildren many things about the Revolutionary War, and particularly about General Washington. Some of these stories would not do to print, especially about the freedom with which 'The Father of his Country' used the English language. But in his estimation no mortal man ever approximated General Washington as a great military chieftain. Sarah Winston, of Hanover, was the sister of Anthony Winston, of Hanover. She married John Henry and was the mother of Patrick Henry. Capt. Anthony Winston was sheriff of Buckingham county, Virginia, which office at that time was given to the oldest justice of the peace of the county for one term, under the law of Virginia. At that time a justice of the peace in Virginia received no pay, the principal business of that officer being to settle disputes among his neighbors without any lawsuit.

"Alice Winston, the mother of Gen. Pettus, was born in Buckingham county, Virginia, but her father moved with his family about the beginning of the last century to Davidson county, Tennessee, and owned a plantation there, about one mile from the Hermitage. John Pettus was born in Fluvanna county, Virginia, near where Anthony Winston lived. He also moved to Davidson county, Tennessee, about the first of the last century. Alice Winston and John Pettus were married in Davidson county in 1807, and General Jackson danced at the wedding. And in the early days of Senator Pettus he was frequently at the 'Hermitage' and heard General Jackson tell of the early life of his mother and father, and of his father's serving in the Creek War under him."—Mrs. P. H. Mell. in *Transactions* of the Alabama Historical Society, Vol. iv, pp. 569-572.

WOOD, JOHN, aged 89, resided in Jackson county, June 1, 1840, with Thomas Campbell.—*Census of Pensioners*, 1841, p. 148.

WOODS, THOMAS, sen., aged 76, and a resident of Dallas county; private of Cavalry S. C. Militia; enrolled on January 30, 1834, under act of Congress of June 7, 1832, payment to date from March 4, 1831; annual allowance, $100; sums received to date of publication of list, $300.—*Revolutionary Pension Roll*, in Vol. xiv, Sen. Doc. 514, 23rd Cong., 1st sess., 1833-34.

WRIGHT, DANIEL, aged 75, and a resident of Madison county; captain N. C. Continental Line and Militia; enrolled on June 12, 1833, under act of Congress of June 7, 1832, payment to date from March 4, 1831; annual allowance, $480; sums received to date of publication of list, $1,200.—*Revolutionary Pension Roll*, in Vol. xiv, Sen. Doc. 514, 23rd Cong., 1st sess., 1833-34.

WRIGHT, JOHN, age not given, a resident of Madison county; private Hamilton's Mounted Gunners; enrolled on December 22, 1831, payment to date from December 15, 1831; annual allowance, $24; April 24, 1816.—*Revolutionary Pension Roll*, in Vol. xiv, Sen. Doc. 514, 23rd Cong., 1st sess., 1833-34. He resided in Madison county, June 1, 1840.—*Census of Pensioners*, 1841, p. 148.

WRIGHT, ROBERT. "ANOTHER REVOLUTIONARY PATRIOT GONE. Departed this life on the 24th inst., ROBERT WRIGHT, SR., a Patriot of the Revolution, aged 85 years and 17 days. He was a native of Amherst county, Virginia—was at the siege of York, and assisted in the capture of Cornwallis. He emigrated to Madison county, Ala., in 1808, where he continued until the day of his death, greatly esteemed and beloved by a large circle of friends and acquaintances..

"The Southern Advocate and Richmond Enquirer are requested to copy."—*The Democrat* (Huntsville), March 21, 1847.

YOUNG, JOHN, aged 90, resided in Wilcox county, June 1, 1840, with Samuel Young.—*Census of Pensioners*, 1841, p. 149.

www.ingramcontent.com/pod-product-compliance
Lightning Source LLC
Chambersburg PA
CBHW020657300426
44112CB00007B/411